Better Homes and Gardens

W9-AAV-294

Complete Guide to
CONTAINER GARDENING

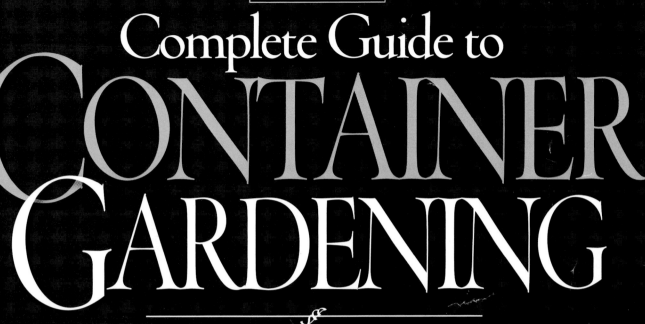

WILEY

John Wiley & Sons, Inc.

Better Homes and Gardens® Complete Guide to Container Gardening
Contributing Writer and Project Editor: Kate Carter Frederick
Contributing Designer: Brad Ruppert
Editor, Garden Books: Denny Schrock
Editorial Assistant: Billie Wade
Contributing Copy Editor: Fran Gardner
Contributing Proofreaders: Sara Henderson, Susan Lang,
    Stephanie Petersen
Contributing Indexer: Ellen Sherron
Contributing Technician: Janet Anderson

Meredith® Books
Editorial Director: Gregory H. Kayko
Editor in Chief, Garden: Doug Jimerson
Editorial Manager: David Speer
Art Director: Tim Alexander
Managing Editor: Doug Kouma
Executive Director, Sales: Ken Zagor
Director, Operations: George A. Susral
Director, Production: Douglas M. Johnston
Business Director: Janice Croat
Vice President and General Manager, SIP: Jeff Myers
Book Production Manager: Doug Johnson
Imaging Center Operator: Jon Pugh

John Wiley & Sons, Inc.
Publisher: Natalie Chapman
Executive Editor: Anne Ficklen
Assistant Editor: Charleen Barila
Production Director: Diana Cisek
Manufacturing Manager: Tom Hyland

Better Homes and Gardens Magazine
Editor in Chief: Gayle Goodson Butler

Meredith Publishing Group
President: Jack Griffin
Excutive Vice President: Doug Olson

Meredith Corporation
Chairman of the Board: William T. Kerr
President and Chief Executive Officer: Stephen M. Lacy

In Memoriam: E.T. Meredith III (1933–2003)

For general information on our other products and services or for
technical support, please contact our Customer Care Department
within the United States at (800) 762–2974, outside the United States
at (317) 572–3993 or fax (317) 572–4002.
Wiley also publishes its books in a variety of electronic formats. Some
content that appears in print may not be available in electronic books.
For more information about Wiley products, visit our web site at
www.wiley.com.

Library of Congress Cataloging-in-Publication Data

Better homes and gardens complete guide to container gardening / by
Better homes and gardens.
p. cm.
Includes index.
ISBN 978-0-470-54030-5 (paper)
1. Container gardening—Handbooks, manuals, etc.
2. Container gardening—Pictorial works. I. Better homes and gardens. II.
Title: Complete guide to container gardening.
SB418.B478 2010   635.9'86—dc22   2009041249

Printed in the United States of America

10 9 8 7 6 5 4 3 2 1

Contents

CHAPTER ONE

Promise in a Pot

A container garden brings character to a patio with pots of tall, showy cannas and bright chrysanthemums along with colorful annuals and houseplants.

For easy-care plantings that bring beauty and versatility to any setting, gardens in containers provide infinite possibilities. All kinds of container gardens can help you enhance your home, set a style, express your personality, tackle your gardening challenges, and improve your quality of life.

Benefits for All

For anyone with dreams of a fabulous garden, hope comes in a container. If you are constrained by time, energy, money, or space, container gardens offer some of the easiest ways to overcome limited resources. For instance, producing a kitchen garden in containers (see page 32) adds to family meals through the summer at a cost of less than a bag of groceries. Although contained plants rely on gardeners for their needs, you can devise a container-tending routine that's enjoyable and suits your everyday life.

Containers provide the ultimate garden accessories: They're colorful, portable, and changeable. Whether you're an experienced gardener or a beginner, potted plantings encourage creative expression and reward it

with cheerful displays that can extend the growing season and even keep going year round.

Count on your potted gardens to generate pleasure and make any setting more appealing. Wherever you live, container gardens allow you to experiment with new plants and combinations. Containers provide opportunities for you to enjoy plants that don't ordinarily grow in your location's climate or soil. Containers can place a garden within comfortable reach and create a garden where there is not enough room or sun for a conventional one. Wherever you put containers to work in your landscape, they'll provide solutions—filling dull or bare spots, marking an entryway, creating privacy, decorating for a party, or keeping produce handy.

right Potted petunias, calibrachoa, coleus, jasmine, and scented geraniums transform a doorstep into a delightfully fragrant garden.

below Pots of purple-leaf coleus and moneywort add color and charm to the hard edge of a patio wall where their repetition unites the containers as part of the landscape design.

opposite Plants can enhance a cheerful entryway. Purple violas, yellow marigolds, and sweet alyssum complement the bright yellow sweet broom (*Cytisus × spachianus)* standards growing companiably in matching urns.

Where to Begin

Start here on your container gardening adventure! This book is designed to lead you through the process, making it easy, enjoyable, and rewarding to plan and plant. Deciding which comes first, the pot or the plant, will be only part of the excitement that comes with creating beautiful container gardens that work with your lifestyle as well as your landscape. You'll soon discover how container gardens improve the look of your home and shape the daily use of your surroundings.

You'll find a trove of ideas and inspiration on the pages ahead. Combining your goals with the seasoned advice offered throughout the book will enable you to make your ideal garden and gain lasting satisfaction from its success. Follow the container "recipes" and complete the step-by-step projects shown or let them inspire your own designs.

Along the way, gather all the tips and techniques you'll need to accomplish your gardening plans. Use the lists of essentials and ingredients on the recipe pages to simplify your plant choices. Then depend on the notes for more in-depth gardening information, suggestions for planting alternatives, and troubleshooting strategies. You'll find a wealth of tips from the experts at the Better Homes and Gardens Test Garden who have tried many of the new plant varieties and planting methods on your behalf.

Before you dig in, see the USDA Plant Hardiness Zone Map on page 218 and identify your zone—that way you can ensure that the plants you choose will be generally suitable to your region's conditions. Determine whether you want a container garden destined for a place that's sunny or shady—or a combination—and make your plans and planting selections on that basis. Let the plant lists throughout the book and the Plant Directory at the back aid you in choosing, planting, and caring for your plants.

Now let the adventure begin! Experiment. See how to turn mistakes into opportunities to learn. Try something different. Throughout the process, reap the joys of container gardening.

top right Urban settings typically leave little room for a garden, but that's where containers often prove most useful. The bright foliage of 'Margarita' sweet potato, licorice plant, and Persian shield in glazed pots and a copper window box stand out against the dark garage.

right A trio of plants—*Caladium* 'Gingerland,' *Begonia* 'Borias,' and *Euphorbia* 'Diamond Frost'—sparkles in a partially shaded spot.

opposite A small porch becomes a cool retreat with the addition of potted plants. The easy-care plantings of bougainvillea, red and yellow crown-of-thorns, and agaves create privacy as well as a pretty view.

CHAPTER TWO

Start with Pots

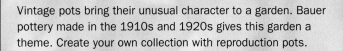

Vintage pots bring their unusual character to a garden. Bauer pottery made in the 1910s and 1920s gives this garden a theme. Create your own collection with reproduction pots.

Finding the ideal pot for a container garden **is almost as much fun as filling it. The best containers not only do their job—holding soil and moisture and helping plants thrive— but also fit your home and garden style. Matching a container to its use makes gardening easier and more satisfying. Start here to find the ideal pot for your garden.**

The Scoop on Pots

As the home for plants, containers provide space for roots to develop and plants to grow and flourish. Any container that holds soil can be used for growing plants, from standard terra-cotta pots to ceramic, metal, wood, and fiberglass planters to old shoes, pasta cookers, wheelbarrows, and hollowed-out logs. Key to your garden's success is the container's ability to provide an adequate growing environment for roots, delivering enough space, moisture, nutrients, and air to nurture them.

If you don't already have containers on hand, you'll soon discover that selection has never been better. You'll find an unlimited array of containers in all materials, sizes, and shapes. They vary in their longevity and ability to provide optimal growing conditions. Ideally, shop where there's a complete selection of containers for you to compare.

The best containers

It pays to buy the best containers you can afford. Poor quality has a way of looking cheap and not lasting. But price does not always equate with quality. Because plants vary in the type of rooting environment they need, you'll want to match the pot to the plants you plan to grow and the environment outside the container. Here's what to look for:

Material Porous materials are good for plants that prefer soil on the dry side and in unexposed sites. Nonporous materials are best for plants that prefer wet conditions or are in hot, sunny, or windy spots. Some container materials, such as terra-cotta, are more porous than others. Ideally the container should not be so porous that water evaporates rapidly from its sides and plantings dry so quickly you need to water several times a day. This can be a problem if the pot is exposed to hot sun, wind, or other drying conditions.

Drainage A drainage hole or other means of releasing excess water is crucial to a plant's survival. Without good drainage, plant roots can suffocate and die. If the container does not come with drainage holes in its bottom, you must create them. Drill one or more holes using a spade bit for plastic or wood, a masonry bit to pierce clay or concrete, or a step bit for metal.

below Plastic pots make it easier than ever to have portable and pretty gardens. They're also easy to clean—a boon to plant health.
below right A magnificent agave stands out in a lush garden thanks to its own architectural strength and the cobalt blue pot that houses it.

Choose containers to suit yourself and the style of your home. There are no rules other than these: Keep it simple and enjoy the process!

Size The larger the container, the more room for roots and the slower soil dries. However, you need to balance the size of the plant with the size of the pot as well as ensure the pot fits the spot you plan to place it in. Also, some plants prefer cramped roots while others require roomy root space.

Large (16 inches or more in diameter), deep pots offer stability and scale and can host large plants and ones with deep or extensive root systems, such as trees and shrubs. The weight of large pots filled with soil, plants, and water limits their portability.

Small (14 inches or less in diameter) or shallow containers suit small or shallow-rooted plants such as bulbs, succulents, and seasonal annuals. Small containers may become a source of frustration if plants outgrow them, and they will need watering more often.

Durability Well-made containers stand up to weather extremes and watering. Unless waterproofed, wet wood tends to rot and wet metal corrodes. Ultraviolet inhibitors protect plastic from sun damage. Sealants minimize damage to metal from fertilizer salts. Some clay pots are guaranteed frostproof by their manufacturers. Wood, polystyrene (foam), and concrete containers help insulate their contents from weather extremes.

Other criteria Some container materials, such as concrete, insulate roots from hot and cold temperatures, a benefit in exposed locations. Dark-colored pots absorb heat; in exposed locations, soil dries quickly and roots suffer in the heat and dryness. What's more, lightweight containers can be moved easily, but heavy ones are less likely to topple in strong winds.

Special containers

In addition to terra-cotta, wood, and other traditional pots and planters, you'll find endless prospects to handle a special job or challenge your imagination.

Self-watering containers feature a built-in reservoir that allows plants to draw moisture as needed and minimize watering chores.

Wall pots are essentially half containers with flat backs that fit up against a wall.

Strawberry pots offer several pockets for planting along their sides.

above Large wall pots are less likely than smaller ones to dry out between waterings.

opposite top To avoid creating a hodgepodge, group containers that have something in common, such as size, shape, color, or texture.

opposite bottom The pockets of a strawberry pot can hold plants other than strawberries— succulents are one possibility.

It's better to have fewer, larger pots than many little ones scattered about, especially in a small space. This potted garden includes a shrub rose and annuals.

Material Matters

Get the most from your containers by understanding the advantages and drawbacks of the materials from which they're made.

1. Terra-cotta or fired clay is either unglazed and porous or glazed and less porous. Heavy when filled with wet soil, it can chip, crack, and break. Because terra-cotta absorbs water, it may crack during freeze-thaw cycles in winter. Low-quality pots easily scratch and chip. High-fired pots are stronger.

2. Concrete, stone, and cast stone excel for durability and elegance. These dense, heavy materials insulate plants from weather extremes, providing a year-round container option, but they are gut-busters to move. And they are expensive. As concrete and stone age, they develop a patina, which lends character.

3. Synthetic containers made of fiberglass, plastic, foam, or other resins are lightweight, easy to clean, and nonporous. Coming in countless shapes, sizes, colors, and textures, their finishes resemble stone, concrete, or other high-end materials at a lower cost. Fiberglass pots can chip or crack. They are poor insulators, as are thin-walled plastic pots. But plastics can be long lasting. Pots marked UV resistant crack and fade less.

4. Metals, such as galvanized metal, cast iron, and copper, offer versatile style and long life. Shiny metal surfaces usually fade into subtle patinas unless they're powder coated, painted, or polished. Water and fertilizers can corrode metal. Treating the inside of the container with a rust inhibitor can extend the life of the pot. Zinc and aluminum won't rust. Metal pots are nonporous; their weight depends on which metal is used and the size of the container.

5. Wooden containers range from rugged half barrels to window boxes and patio planters. Minimally affected by heat and cold, wood insulates roots from wide temperature swings. Choose pressure-treated wood, sustainable hardwood, or rot-resistant cedar or cypress. Relatively nonporous, wooden containers can be left outside year round.

6. Ceramic containers are similar to terra-cotta with the same pros and cons but are made from a different type of clay. Most are glazed and comparatively heavy.

Pot Styles

Sure, you can say it with flowers, but the pots you choose also express your gardening style. The most appropriate containers suit your home and garden with their colors, textures, shapes, and styles. Once you find them, your favorite pots will reward you year after year, adding to your garden's beauty and success.

Colorful pots bring energy to green space and call for exuberant planting.

Earthy pots meld easily with most landscapes; weathered finishes enhanced with rust or moss complement naturalistic plantings.

Sculptural shapes, clean lines, and symmetry lend sophistication to classic containers.

Simple pots let plants dominate. For more decorative effects, choose colorful, ornate, or otherwise showy containers.

If you're like most gardeners, you head to the garage at the first sign of spring, pull out all the pots, and start wondering what to put in them. This glossary of container styles can help you match your plantings to your pots.

Bowls are squat containers with rounded sides. They may or may not have a foot. Low-profile plants look best in bowls, as do plantings that give a rounded top to the bowl.

Troughs are long, shallow square or rectangular planters, often with a rough or rustic surface. They are frequently used for growing alpine plants, succulents, and other shallow-rooted low growers.

Pans refer to squatty standard pots, less tall than they are wide. Often called azalea pots, bulb pans, or seed pans, they pair well with low-profile plants.

Long toms, also called rose pots, are about two or more times taller than wide and flared at the lip. Plants should be twice the height of the container to be in scale with the pot. Include a cascading plant for a proportional effect.

Square pots may be modern or classic in looks depending on how the container is decorated

above right Hefty concrete containers typically stay put, becoming a permanent part of a site and reinforcing its traditional style.

right A terra-cotta bowl benefits from its lofty placement on a tree stump. It could be planted with lettuce or succulents for equally pleasing results.

opposite Cast-stone or concrete troughs can be difficult to lift and move, so choose their destination carefully.

and planted. A pot with straight, clean lines and little decoration feels contemporary. Letting foliage spill over the edge softens its lines for a homier look. Highly decorated containers with simple plantings complement traditional schemes.

Standard pots are equally deep and wide but broader at their top than their base. This is the most common shape for containers. The even proportions complement most plantings and ensure stability. More decorative versions of standard pots are sometimes called vases. The larger the pot, the more or the larger the plants it will hold. Ideally, keep the planting about two times the height of the container.

Cylinders and other geometric shapes present a modern appearance. A simple scheme with one striking architectural plant especially complements such containers.

Urns are bowl- or vase-shape containers with flared lips on footed pedestals. They're classic containers with a formal shape that looks good in traditional gardens with single or mixed plantings.

Jars have broad shoulders and narrow necks. They are sophisticated looking, especially with a long slinky plant trailing over the rim of jar. However, their shape is one of the most difficult to match with plantings. Because of their small openings, it's difficult for the plants growing in them to get adequate oxygen to their roots.

above The earthy texture and porosity of terra-cotta make it ideal for a wide range of plants from fiber-optic grass (*Isolepsis cernua*) to succulent echeveria.
opposite A very large and beautifully glazed jar gives a special plant such as *Melianthus comosus* the stellar treatment it deserves. Planting succulents in small pots at its feet highlights the display.

BHG
CONTAINER
BASICS

WEATHERIZE CONTAINERS Baskets, wooden boxes, and some other containers quickly disintegrate when exposed to wet soil; metal rusts. To help preserve the integrity of your containers, plant in plastic pots that fit inside them. To protect the exterior of vulnerable containers, apply several coats of exterior waterproofing sealant to wooden, woven, and some metallic vessels. You can also transform ordinary terra-cotta pots into fun, colorful accents in minutes with exterior oil-based acrylic paint, but this will not seal or waterproof the containers.

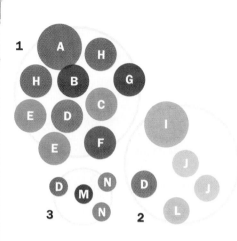

Essentials
Container: 14-inch glazed earthenware pots and 20-inch bowl
Light: Sun
Water: When soil begins to feel dry

Ingredients
Pot 1
A. 1 switch grass (*Panicum virgatum* 'Cloud Nine')
B. 1 coleus ('Saturn')
C. 1 fancy-leaf geranium ('Crystal Palace Gem')
D. 1 golden Japanese sedum ('Ogon')
E. 2 Queen Victoria century plant
F. 1 hen-and-chicks
G. 1 creeping wire vine
H. 2 lotus vine ('Amazon Sunset')

Pot 2
I. 1 giant echeveria
J. 2 ghost echeveria
D. 1 golden Japanese sedum ('Ogon')
L. 1 ice plant

Pot 3
M. 1 variegated agave ('Variegata')
D. 1 golden Japanese sedum
N. 2 yellow crooked sedum ('Angelina')

Notes
The similarities of these pots' finishes and overall appearances relate them as a group. If you design your pots individually, group those with similar features to multiply their impact.

Glazed Expression

Containers of glazed earthenware—a porous ceramic—fit almost any garden style. Their rich, deep colors spread a garden's vitality to an entry where they draw people in. The flat bowl in the foreground is a vintage pot from Thailand. Check importers, antique stores, and specialty potteries for similar containers.

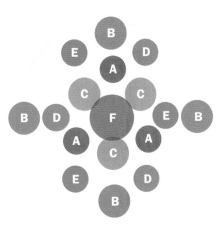

Essentials

Container: 16-inch acid green glazed ceramic bowl
Light: Sun
Water: Keep soil moist

Ingredients

A. 3 pansy ('Ultima Baron Merlot')
B. 4 lettuce ('Esmeralda')
C. 3 ornamental cabbage ('Pigeon Red')
D. 3 viola ('Sorbet Primrose Babyface')
E. 3 viola ('Sorbet Yellow Delight')
F. 1 chives

Notes

In early summer, discard the lettuce and transplant the ornamental cabbage and chives to your garden, where they'll have space to mature. Replant the bowl with a selection of compact warm-season edibles for salads, such as carrot ('Parmex Baby Ball', 'Little Finger', or 'Tiny Sweet'), beet ('Little Ball' or 'Little Chicago'), and globe basil.

SUMMER GREENS

Continue to harvest fresh greens into summer. Hot weather typically spells an end to cool-season greens. Plant varieties that are heat tolerant or slow to bolt (set seed). Move the container to a shadier, cooler location when temperatures warm.

SUN

Salad Bowl

Toss together a big bowl of cool-season edibles, including tender lettuce, violas, and pansies for garden-fresh spring salads. Sow lettuce seeds for a harvest in about 50 days, or go with nursery-started seedlings to enjoy your first harvest in half that time.

Essentials

Container: 14-inch square terra-cotta pots
Light: Sun
Water: When the soil begins to feel dry

Ingredients

A. 4 yellow French marigold
B. 4 orange French marigold
C. 4 mahogany red French marigold

Notes

Square containers hold more soil than cylindrical ones of the same diameter. So if you're trying to decide whether to put long-term plantings of perennials, vegetables, or shrubs in a 12-inch square pot or a 12-inch standard pot, the square one will better meet their needs. The containers in this garden are set in square saucers to avoid staining the wood and pavers.

TEST GARDEN TIP

MERRY MARIGOLDS

Easy-to-grow French marigolds are stocky, bushy annuals, 8 to 16 inches tall. Their 2-inch yellow, orange, red-orange, or mahogany blooms perfectly complement terra-cotta pots. Plants bloom from early summer to fall, especially if you maintain consistent soil moisture and snap off the spent flowers. Keep an eye out for spider mites.

Step It Up

The repetition of color and shape reinforces the rhythm of a garden, here turning ordinary steps into strong features. Using just one type of plant and pot unifies the design and keeps the sense of rhythm going step by step.

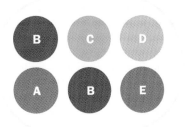

Essentials

Container: 10×10×18-inch basket
Light: Sun
Water: When the soil begins to feel dry

Ingredients

A. 1 snapdragon ('Playful Ice')
B. 2 trailing peach verbena
C. 1 coleus ('Glennis')
D. 1 licorice plant
E. 1 zinnia ('Zahara Yellow')

Notes

Line the container with a moisture-holding basket liner or landscape fabric. The liner will help hold in the potting mix. Apply at least two coats of clear, outdoor-type sealant to the inside and outside of a woven container before planting to help it shrug off moisture and withstand wet weather.

CONTAINER BASICS

NEW & IMPROVED

When you try newly developed plant varieties introduced each year, you'll discover opportunities for exciting plant combinations. Scan mail order seed and plant catalogs, visit garden centers, and view websites of your favorite plant purveyors to keep tabs on what's new and improved.

SUN

Sunny Side Up

Starting with new varieties of dependable annuals such as zinnia and snapdragon elevates a container garden to something special. Choosing a creative container adds flair to your garden. Display the garden by setting the container on bricks to keep it off the ground.

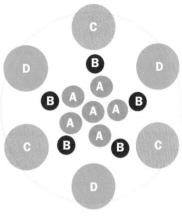

Ol' Ironsides

Cast-iron containers like this Victorian birdbath prove their strength and durability by outliving generations of gardeners. Classic among planters, they look great when filled with favorite annuals for a traditional display especially suited to a historical setting.

Essentials

Container: 24-inch cast-iron planter
Light: Sun
Water: As needed to keep soil damp

Ingredients

A. 6 annual salvia ('Victoria Blue')
B. 5 geranium ('Global Red')
C. 3 lantana ('White Weeping')
D. 3 licorice plant ('Limelight')

Notes

Cast iron stands up to freezing temperatures. In fall replant cast-iron containers with cold-hardy plants or fill with evergreen boughs. If you seek the dependability of cast iron but prefer a planter in a modern style, check large garden centers and the Resources list on page 219.

CONTAINER BASICS

PLANT IN PLACE

Containers made from heavy materials such as cast iron are extremely difficult to move when filled with wet soil. Set the pot into place, then plant. Drainage is essential, so if a cast-iron planter lacks a drainage hole, treat it as a cachepot. Plant in a drainable pot, then set it on a layer of large gravel inside the cast-iron vessel.

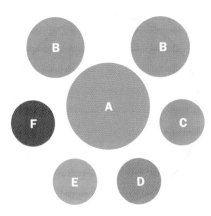

Essentials

Container: 20-inch glazed urn
Light: Sun
Water: When soil begins to feel dry

Ingredients

A. 1 dwarf citrus
B. 2 trailing rosemary ('Prostratus')
C. 1 blue oat grass ('Sapphire')
D. 1 oregano
E. 1 blue fescue
F. 1 common sage ('Tricolor')

Notes

Underplantings give a potted tree more dimension and personality. Here, herbs and grasses soften the pot's edge without taking attention from the citrus tree. It's easy to replace the underplantings each year, using the same varieties or different ones.

CONTAINER BASICS

TWICE AS NICE

When potting a tree or shrub, choose a container at least twice the width and depth of the plant's root ball. This will give it enough room for healthy growth from the roots up.

SUN

Treasure Trove

Special plants call for extraordinary containers and vice versa. This elegant urn with an unusual glazed finish suits a small citrus tree. The pot's depth and heft can hold a dwarf tree for several years before it requires repotting.

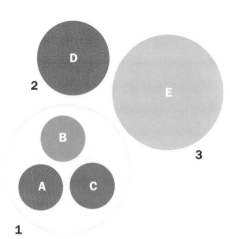

2

D

E

3

B

A

C

1

Essentials
Container: 18×24 to 20×48-inch stone pots
Light: Sun
Water: When the soil dries

Ingredients
Pot 1
A. 1 garlic chives
B. 1 flat-leaf parsley
C. 1 common sage ('Tricolor')

Pot 2
D. 1 mint

Pot 3
E. 1 thyme ('Silver Queen')

Notes
This group of planters shows how age adds patina to stone and brings elegance to the gathering. Substitute your favorite herbs and a cohesive group of cast-stone containers. Herbs benefit from the quick-draining and -drying conditions in porous cast-stone, concrete, and terra-cotta pots. Giving plants plenty of room to develop in ample-size pots cinches their success.

DID YOU KNOW?

WATERING LESS
Reduce how often you need to water plants growing in unglazed pots by grouping them so their sides are sheltered as much as possible from the evaporative effects of sun and wind.

Set in Stone

Large cast-stone or concrete planters offer a long-term home for perennial herbs. The heavy-duty containers' thick walls insulate roots from extremes of heat and cold. The perennial herbs will be sustainable in the pots year after year where the climate allows.

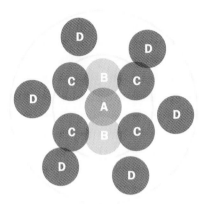

Essentials

Container: Salvaged or new chicken feeder
Light: Sun
Water: When soil begins to feel dry

Ingredients

A. 1 sedge ('Toffee Twist')
B. 2 *Euphorbia* ('Diamond Frost')
C. 4 creeping wire vine
D. 6 hen-and-chicks ('Silverline')

Notes

Keep the chicken feeder—or any other found object used as a container—in good shape from year to year by sealing it with two coats of water-resistant exterior polyurethane. Display this unusual container in a garden bed where it will surprise and delight visitors.

GARDENERS' GOLD MINE

If one person's junk is another's treasure, just think of the great finds to be unearthed at yard sales, thrift shops, and flea markets. Functional objects gleaned from odds and ends await transformation into funky and fun container gardens.

PURINA
P-32G
TUBE FEEDER
GROWING-LAYING

PURINA
QUALITY

RALSTON PURINA COMPANY

Playing Chicken

Whether recently purchased or salvaged from the trash, an unconventional container such as this galvanized chicken feeder has playful appeal and gives a garden instant personality.

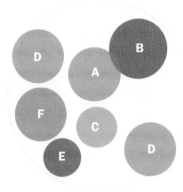

Treasured Cache

Antique crocks and other heavy-duty stoneware pieces collecting dust in your basement or garage make excellent planters. Protect the items' value by using them as seasonal cachepots rather than drilling drainage holes.

Essentials

Container: 12-gallon stoneware crock; inner plastic pot to fit
Light: Sun
Water: When soil feels dry. Empty excess water from the crock.

Ingredients

A. 1 blue oat grass
B. 1 switch grass ('Shenandoah')
C. 1 common sage ('Tricolor')
D. 2 myrtle spurge
E. 1 purple petunia
F. 1 purple aster ('Sungal')

Notes

Watering can leave rusty-looking calcium deposits on the inside and outside of containers, even when they are used as cachepots. To prevent calcium deposits on valuable containers, line them with plastic sheeting. Pot plants in a utilitarian plastic container; slip it into the crock, then trim the sheeting to the crock's rim. Empty the crock and store it indoors before the weather turns cold.

PLANT SWAP

ALTERNATIVE PLANTINGS

For a similar effect, try blue oatgrass, ornamental oregano ('Kent Beauty'), October daphne stonecrop, lavender chrysanthemum, and 'Lady in Black' aster.

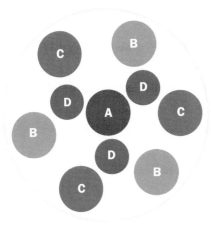

Essentials

Container: 18-inch plastic urn
Materials: Stone-finish spray paint;
48-inch obelisk
Light: Sun
Water: Keep soil moist

Ingredients

A. 1 creeping gloxinia
(*Lophospermum* 'Great Cascade
Wine Red')
B. 3 mini petunia ('Whispers
Appleblossom')
C. 3 verbena ('Escapade Bright Eye')
D. 3 coleus ('Trailing Plum')

Notes

Gently guide the creeping gloxinia
to climb the obelisk, where it will
stand out in the center of the
container. Pinch off the ends of
the petunias and coleus when
they reach 4 to 6 inches tall to
encourage bushy growth and
better blooming.

CONTAINER BASICS

A NEW COAT

Transform an inexpensive
plastic container, giving it
the appearance of textured
stone, with a little spray paint.
Find stone-look finishes at
a hardware store. Once dry,
protect the finish by topping
it with a coat of exterior
polyurethane.

Puttin' on the Ritz

Who would guess that an ordinary plastic
urn could become an extraordinary container
garden with a few simple steps. Add paint,
a plant support, and plants to complete
the makeover.

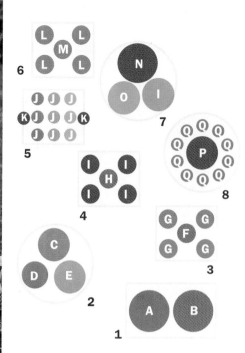

Handy Harvest

Fresh, tender greens and a bounty of organic salad makings grow within easy reach, no matter what size yard you have. Begin by rescuing gently used wooden crates and spacious baskets. Paint them for a coordinated look.

Essentials

Container: Repurposed wooden crates (produce or wine boxes); baskets. Landscape fabric or moisture-retentive basket liner
Light: Sun to partial shade
Water: Daily, if needed, to keep soil from drying out

Ingredients

Box 1
A. beet
B. carrot

Basket 2
C. thyme
D. chives
E. pepper

Box 3
F. Swiss chard
G. calendula

Box 4
H. tomato
I. basil

Box 5
J. lettuce
K. malabar spinach

Box 6
L. cabbage
M. marigold

Basket 7
N. tomato
O. parsley
I. basil

Basket 8
P. cucumber
Q. onion

Notes

Cultivate the produce you enjoy most for your daily meals. If you crave little more than greens, grow spinach, kale, chard, and varieties of lettuce in pretty patchworks.

Shallow-rooted vegetables such as lettuces, dwarf carrots, and beets get by in soil 4 inches deep.

step 1

step 2

HERE'S HOW...

1 Pick your planters

Choose wooden crates and baskets big enough to hold the soil and moisture necessary to sustain mature plants—the larger, the better. To hold the soil, line containers with landscape fabric or water-retentive basket liner.

2 Combine compatible plants

Group plants with similar needs, such as sun-loving globe basil and a petite pepper, in each container. Most vegetables and herbs grow best in a location with at least 6 hours of sun daily, but they can vary in their need for water and fertilizer. Pair vegetables with herbs or edible flowers for an interesting display.

3 Mulch to minimize your work

Spread a ½- to 1-inch layer of cocoa bean shells or other mulch over the soil's surface to help preserve soil moisture. Water thoroughly after planting.

Raise containers on steps, bricks, or other platforms for easier picking and care.

step 3

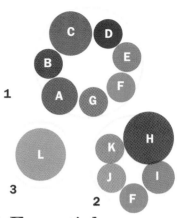

Essentials

Container: 8-, 12-, and 14-inch glazed pots
Light: Part shade
Water: When soil begins to feel dry

Ingredients

Pot 1
A. 1 chartreuse sweet potato ('Margarita')
B. 1 yellow-edge red coleus ('Volcano')
C. 1 hibiscus ('Maple Sugar')
D. 1 dark purple alternanthera ('Gail's Choice')
E. 1 multicolored coleus ('Mt. Washington')
F. 1 sweet potato ('Black Heart')
G. 1 heuchera ('Strike It Rich Pink Gem')

Pot 2
H. 1 Bauer's dracaena ('Red Star Spike')
I. 1 heuchera ('Dolce Crème Brûlée')
F. 1 sweet potato ('Black Heart')
J. 1 moneywort ('Goldilocks')
K. 1 diascia ('Flying Colors Trailing Red')

Pot 3
L. 1 leatherleaf sedge

Notes

Aiming for a diverse collection of foliage with purple or chartreuse aspects results in a unified effect. Tall or deep pots allow long-season root growth.

Unity in Diversity

Packed with fancy foliage, long tom containers capture attention and say welcome. Mixing tall and trailing plants maximizes this leafy garden's effect as it enlivens a shaded entryway with its striking composition.

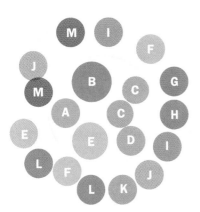

Essentials

Container: 12-inch terra-cotta long tom; 24-inch lightweight terra-cotta-look pot
Light: Part shade
Water: Keep soil damp

Ingredients

Top pot
A. 1 yellow-leaf hosta ('Stained Glass')
B. 1 red fountain grass ('Rubrum')
C. 2 kale ('Nagoya Rose')
D. 1 moneywort ('Aurea')
E. 1 red-leaf sedum ('Sunset Cloud')

Bottom pot
E. 1 red-leaf sedum ('Sunset Cloud')
F. 2 pink daisy mum
G. 1 orange sedge
H. 1 Swiss chard ('Bright Lights')
I. 2 pink-and-yellow snapdragon
J. 2 moneywort ('Golden Globe')
K. 1 heuchera ('Palace Purple')
L. 2 pansy ('Icicle')
M. 2 orange mum ('Ashley')

Notes

To make this tower, simply snuggle a long tom or a tall standard pot into the soil of a larger, broader container. Help secure it by pushing a bamboo garden stake through the top pot's drain hole into the larger pot below it. Add plants and you're ready to step back and enjoy the season-extending show.

PART SHADE

Welcome Committee

Terra-cotta pots are the perfect color accompaniment to fall plantings. Let them be the centerpiece of your autumn decorations in this welcoming tower of seasonal plants and colors.

Essentials
Container: 10-inch round hypertufa pot; 14-inch hypertufa bowl
Light: Part shade
Water: When soil feels dry

Ingredients
Pot 1
A. 1 ornamental oregano ('Kent Beauty')

Bowl 2
B. 1 blue onion
C. 1 boxwood ('Morris Midget')
D. 1 ajuga ('Metallica Crispa')
E. 1 creeping thyme
F. 1 hen-and-chicks
G. 1 *Dianthus nitidus*
1 small to medium stone

Notes
Earthy hypertufa pots can be purchased or made at home from a mix of Portland cement, perlite, and peat moss. Creating them yourself is fun. The process allows you to make containers in any size or shape desired.

DID YOU KNOW?

WINTER HARDINESS
You can leave hypertufa containers outdoors through cold winters, as long as you move them to a protected spot, out of the sun, and cover them with a pile of evergreen boughs. This protects the plants, as well as the container, from damage caused by freeze-thaw cycles.

Stone Wannabes

Stone-look hypertufa is a long-lasting, porous, and lightweight material. It makes an ideal container for plants that require ample drainage and aeration. Succulents, herbs, alpines, and rock garden plants highlight hypertufa bowls and troughs as much as the pots show off the plants.

Essentials

Container: 3-, 4-, and 6-inch square copper pots; copper tray
Light: Part shade
Water: Keep soil moist

Ingredients

A. 1 lemon cypress topiary
(*Cupressus macrocarpa* 'Wilma')
B. 1 alpine lady's mantle
(*Alchemilla alpina*)
C. 1 rosemary topiary (*Rosmarinus officinalis* 'Tuscan Blue')
D. 1 Yellow Scotch moss (*Sagina subulata* 'Aurea')

Notes

Line the copper tray with sheet moss (from a crafts store) to protect it from scratches. Pour off any water that accumulates in the tray. Trim the topiaries to maintain their tidy appearance.

CONTAINER BASICS

LITTLE ONES

Small pots less than 8 inches in diameter work best as temporary homes for small plants that need nurturing. Placing pint-size plantings on a tabletop helps you keep an eye on them and tend to their needs. Transplant specimens into larger pots as need be.

A Walk in the Park

Solitary plantings gain impact when grouped. Gather eyecatching plants into a serene tablescape, using copper pots and handfuls of tumbled stones to highlight them on a tray.

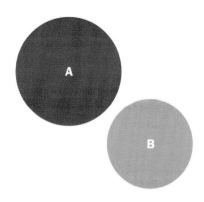

Essentials

Container: Clay chimney liners of various diameters, lengths, and shapes
Tools: Circular saw with carbide blade
Light: Part shade
Water: When soil begins to feel dry

Ingredients

A. Bauer's dracaena (*Cordyline baueri*)
B. pink vinca

Notes

Purchase chimney liners from chimney repair businesses, building supply stores, or Internet sources. Use a circular saw with a carbide blade to cut the round or square liners to the desired height. If you want to paint your chimney liners, use an exterior-grade paint.

CONTAINER BASICS

WINTER PROTECTION

Because they're made from porous clay, chimney liners should be moved to dry, frost-free storage during winter in cold climates, to protect them from temperature extremes. Return the chimney liners to the garden in spring when the weather warms.

Columns of Color

Transform inexpensive clay chimney liners into contemporary containers. Employ their natural looks or customize them to suit your landscape with a quick coat of paint.

When planting the container and using it in a garden bed, this step is unnecessary.

step 1

step 2

HERE'S HOW...

1 Add a bottom

Prevent soil from washing out of the liner when you water the plants. Cut a piece of landscape fabric to the size of the bottom opening. Attach it to the planter using construction adhesive. Be aware: The fabric won't hold the weight of the potting mix if you pick up the planter.

2 Plant directly in the liner

Position the chimney liner where you plan to display it all summer, then fill it with soil and add plants. Situate chimney liners alone or in a group.

3 Or use as cachepot

Set plants still in their nursery pots into the liners. A gallon-size pot fits inside a 7½- to 8-inch-diameter liner.

Chimney liners make great planters. Also use them to display garden decor.

step 3

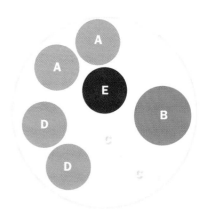

Essentials
Container: 10-inch glazed pot
Light: Part shade to sun
Water: As needed to keep
soil damp

Ingredients
A. 2 night-scented stock
B. 1 flowering kale
C. 2 white pansy
D. 2 pansy ('Matrix Rose Blotch')
E. 1 china pink (*Dianthus chinensis*)

Notes
Treat yourself to a new container as the gardening season approaches. It's bound to inspire delightful plantings. If a new pot isn't in your budget, give new life to an old pot with a coat of glossy exterior paint.

CONTAINER BASICS

POTS WITH POLISH
Glazed ceramic pots cost considerably more than unglazed terra-cotta ones, but they offer a range of color choices. Although glazed pots don't dry out as quickly, they can chip easily.

Bright & Early
A pot of cold-tolerant annuals provides an encouraging preview of spring long before the last frost and the garden's first flowers. These bedding plants are often available at garden centers for fall planting too.

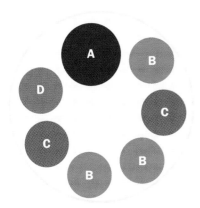

Essentials

Container: 16-inch cast-iron urn
Light: Part shade
Water: Keep soil damp

Ingredients

A. 1 purple fountain grass ('Rubrum')
B. 3 lobelia ('Royal Jewels')
C. 2 moneywort ('Aurea')
D. 1 vinca vine

Notes

Include a tall plant such as 36-inch-tall purple fountain grass in a tall container to maximize its impact. A tall plant or two will contribute balance as well as height to a container garden.

AIM HIGH

Achieve height in a container garden using ornamental grasses, tropicals (hibiscus, canna, elephant's ear), or architectural plants (yucca, agave, New Zealand flax).

Tall, Dark & Handsome

A vaselike urn boasts classic elegance that never goes out of style. Nearly indestructible, a cast-iron container harmonizes with most settings and plants.

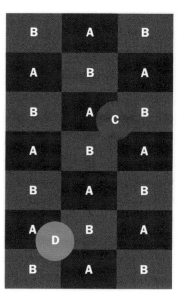

Tic-Tac-Trough

A faux-stone trough has a rugged, time-worn appearance even when new. This one holds a mossy checkerboard that serves as a platform for small potted plants. The wee plant selections might otherwise get lost among larger plants in a garden bed.

Essentials

Container: 15×32-inch hypertufa trough; two 5-inch pots
Light: Part shade to sun
Water: Keep the moss consistently moist; let the two potted plants dry slightly before watering

Ingredients

A. 10 green Scotch moss
B. 11 yellow Scotch moss ('Aurea')
C. 1 dwarf conifer
D. 1 hen-and-chicks

Notes

Troughs made of stone, concrete, or a lighter-weight material called hypertufa draw people to appreciate their contents. Creeping alpines, succulents, and rock garden plants especially suit their low profile.

BHG TEST GARDEN TIP

MOSSY CHECKERBOARD

Plant contrasting varieties of Scotch moss to create an instant checkerboard effect. Trim the moss as needed every few weeks using grass clippers or scissors to maintain the pattern.

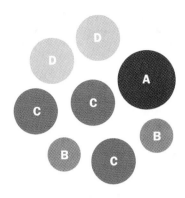

Essentials

Container: 20-inch synthetic pot
Light: Shade
Water: Keep soil moist

Ingredients

A. 1 sword fern
B. 2 English ivy
C. 3 impatiens ('Swirl Pink')
D. 2 caladium ('Candidum')

Notes

When it comes to summer bulbs such as caladium, the bigger the bulb, the bigger the plant. Because summer bulbs take warmth, sun, and a month or two to really get growing, buy them in 6-inch or larger pots for instant impact. If you start with small plants, mass them in groups of three or more for the best effect.

CONTAINER BASICS

MEASURE UP

Somehow, containers always seem big enough at the store when you decide to purchase them, but when you bring them home, they appear smaller in their surroundings. Prevent this common problem by taking along measurements when shopping. Note the height of deck rails, width of landings, or dimensions of other places where containers may be displayed.

Big & Bold

Why wait months for slow-growing plants to fill a pot—especially in shade, where their impact may be needed most? Get the biggest effect possible in the least amount of time by planting a large container with premium-size annuals and summer-flowering bulbs.

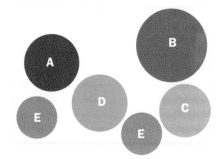

Essentials

Container: 14×22×10-inch salvaged wooden crate
Light: Shade
Water: Keep soil damp

Ingredients

A. 1 caladium
B. 1 schefflera
C. 1 polka-dot plant
D. 1 Persian shield
E. 2 variegated Algerian ivy

Notes

The built-in handles of this sturdy crate make it easy to tote the container wherever you want. All plants can remain in their individual containers. Gradually expose them to new digs with bright natural sunlight to avoid burning the leaves. Move the plants back inside before chilly weather returns in fall.

CAN-DO DESIGN

EYE ON THE PRIZE

Highlight a container garden by placing it at eye level, where it will attract attention. An overturned crate or a substantial pot makes a handy yet stylish pedestal.

Temporary Tenants

A jazzy arrangement of striking foliage plants in a wooden crate brightens any shady spot. Consider houseplants when stocking your container garden. You'll find dozens of selections with colorful foliage and tropical texture to round out your displays.

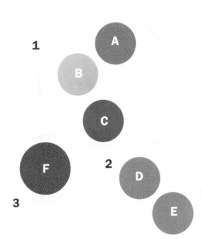

Essentials
Container: 10-, 12-, and 16-inch galvanized metal pots
Light: Shade
Water: Keep soil moist

Ingredients
Pot 1
A. 1 perilla ('Gage's Shadow')
B. 1 caladium ('Florida Elise')
C. 1 purple-leaf heuchera

Pot 2
D. 1 New Guinea impatiens ('Sonic Cherry')
E. 1 oxalis ('Zinfandel')

Pot 3
F. 1 pony tail fern (*Asparagus densiflorus* 'Myers')

Notes
A triangular grouping of containers often ensures a display's success. Use the largest container as the apex or anchor of the group, setting it in the center or to one side. Cluster the rest of the containers around it, contrasting them by height or width to strike a balance.

Shining in Shade

Plantings that show off a bonanza of bright colors and interesting or contrasting textures stand out in shade. Gleaming metallic containers reflect light, making them veritable beacons that stand out along with the plants.

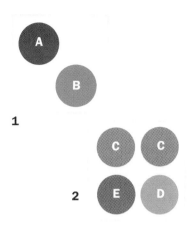

1

2

Essentials

For two containers:
Six 12×12-inch pavers
Five 8×16-inch pavers
Two 8×8-inch pavers
Materials: Landscape block
adhesive; caulking gun
Light: Shade
Water: Keep soil moist

Ingredients

Planter 1
A. 1 elephant's ear ('Black Magic')
B. 1 alocasia

Planter 2
C. 2 coleus ('Inky Fingers')
D. 1 chartreuse hosta
E. 1 oshima sedge ('Evergold')

Notes

When attaching the bottom of the
planter, use drops of adhesive
rather than a solid bead. This
leaves channels through which
water can drain.

Square Root of Two

CAN-DO DESIGN

Let's face it: Containers can be expensive.
These two, however, cost less than $20 to make
yet are as stylish as pots costing fives times
that amount. Assembling them takes little
time and few materials.

SPACE MAKER
Put together at least two
planters. Using similar elements
throughout a landscape creates a
coherence that's easy on the eye
and helps the elements—in this
case, the planters—integrate into
their setting. Also, you can give
a small space a sense of greater
dimension by using two or more
planters of contrasting sizes.

Concrete is heavy to lift. Make the planters near their planting site.

step 1

step 2

HERE'S HOW...

1 Form the sides

Stand four pavers on edge to make a square. Tilt one paver back and apply a bead of adhesive along the left and right inside edges. Press the paver against its neighbors to secure. Repeat on the opposite paver. Adjust the pavers to form a true square.

2 Attach the bottom

Apply drops of adhesive to the exposed edges of the pavers. Set the remaining paver on top; make sure all sides are straight.

3 Set the planters in place

After 24 hours you can move the planters to your garden. Take care, though—the glue is not fully cured for five to seven days. To raise the planters off the ground, set them on the remaining pavers.

Add color to the planter using concrete stain, if you like.

step 3

CHAPTER THREE

Focus on Plants

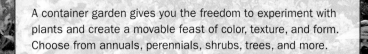

A container garden gives you the freedom to experiment with plants and create a movable feast of color, texture, and form. Choose from annuals, perennials, shrubs, trees, and more.

The surest way to make container gardens with knockout good looks **is to focus on the plants you put in them. Whether you seek lasting color for an outdoor space or want to make a statement that is fabulous and fun, it's the plants that make it happen. Put plants to work and discover which ones perform best for you.**

Selecting Plants

Choosing plants for containers is as easy as picking up a flat of petunias at the garden center. You might shop with a list of favorites in mind, such as the butterhead lettuce and basil that are essential to your summer meals or the dwarf yellow marigolds that work best in those square pots on the front steps. You might head to the garden center with just a color scheme in the back of your mind. Or maybe you just like to be surprised by what you find at the store.

As you browse the nursery aisles, you'll find a familiar group of candidates available year after year that have growth habits and requirements well suited to life in your region's climate. These have proven reliable for quick color and good looks, especially in combination with

one another. You will also find an amazingly wide world of new planting possibilities—a continually expanding array of new and improved varieties. If you let them, these newcomers will inspire your planting schemes and take your containers from pretty good to gorgeous.

Your ideal plants

Generally, almost any plant can grow successfully in a container, at least for a limited time, as long as you meet its needs for light, water, and nutrients. But determining the best plants for your garden depends on your goals.

Before you start picking out plants, think about what you want to accomplish. Do you seek colorful plantings with the longest season and the least maintenance? Perhaps you wish to dress up your deck or patio with a few big pots of bold foliage for a special event. Or maybe you want to brighten a shady spot in the yard, decorate a dull fence, or transform a small backyard for fall. You'll find plants to address these goals and more.

A trip to your local greenhouse or nursery offers an exciting way to discover ideal candidates for containers. The plant colors, names, and prospects prove dazzling—and dizzying—even for the most advanced gardeners. Enjoy the kid-in-a-candy-store feeling, then step back and apply the guidelines on the following pages to make choosing easier.

opposite Switch grass *(Panicum virgatum)* in tall blue pots accents containers of cascading calibrachoa, bright coleus, classic geranium, and *Artemisia stelleriana* 'Silver Brocade'.
right An unusual container of purple pineapple lily *(Eucomis* 'Sparkling Burgundy') draws attention to the long-blooming tropical bulb.
below Ever-reliable pots of red geraniums and purple petunias add color and interest to a sunny site, disguising the sharp edges along stairs.

Planting for the Seasons

Most people like the idea of an easy-care garden that looks its best throughout the growing season. A vast selection of plants are available to make big splashes of spring-to-fall color and form in your containers.

The annuals and frost-sensitive perennials also known as bedding plants carry on and on throughout the growing season, producing reams of blooms, foliage, or both. Petunia, salvia, moneywort, and many others are inexpensive enough to buy in quantity, which encourages experimentation. Use the plants generously, then toss them on the compost pile when they pass their prime.

Long-term prospects

Year-round plantings provide the most lasting displays. Many woody plants and hardy perennials will thrive in containers for several years or more as long as the pot is roomy enough to sustain them. Dwarf shrubs and trees work especially well as single-specimen plantings. Select varieties that are at least two zones hardier than your climate and pot them in frost-resistant containers so you can leave them in place over winter. Underplanting with seasonal bedding plants gives the display an extra spark and added color that can last into winter in warm climates.

Temporary tenants

Seasonal plantings jump-start the gardening season in early spring or extend it in fall. Take advantage of the plants that strut their stuff in cool weather by filling pots with them or tucking them around permanent plants. The temporary displays will brighten your world until they peak and give way.

Pansy, viola, dwarf snapdragon, English daisy, and an array of prechilled bulbs (hyacinth, daffodil, tulip) top the list of spring's glorious-but-temporary bloomers. Round out early displays with spring perennials such as primrose, creeping phlox, and forget-me-not. Come fall, cold-hardy pansies, ornamental kale and cabbage, chrysanthemum, and stock, among others, can rejuvenate your waning summer container gardens for a few more pleasureful weeks.

below A well-braced shelf holds wooden tubs of long-season boxwood, purple sweet alyssum, yellow violas, and orange and yellow nasturtiums.
below right Bold mounds of fall-blooming chrysanthemums and leafy kale fill in where spent annuals require replacing late in the growing season.

left This container garden shines on the deck, linking the indoors and outdoors, throughout the summer. It includes crape myrtle standards, variegated shell ginger, 'Inky Toes' coleus, and asparagus fern.

below Celebrate spring by packing a pot with 'Giant Excelsior' stock, pansies, and pussy willow branches. Enjoy the show while it lasts.

Narrowing Your Choices

If you feel overwhelmed by the number of choices at the garden center, simplify the selection by focusing on the practical advantages that come with all kinds of plants. Recognizing a plant's strengths, such as drought tolerance or slow growth, for instance, will help you get the most impact and enjoyment from your container plantings. Look for this information on plant tags, store signage, and in the Plant Directory at the back of this book. You'll discover gradually which plants give you the greatest return on your investment of effort and money.

Plant types

Knowing the type of plant (think annual, perennial, or shrub) gives you clues about how it might behave in a container. A quick look at plant types will help guide your selections.

Annual plants complete their life cycle in one growing season. They come in a range of colors and forms. Plants that are perennial in warm climates are used as annuals in cooler climates where they're not hardy.

Perennials are a vast group ranging from diminutive groundcovers to large-leaf wonders that return and grow larger each year. Some offer fabulous seasonal flowers; others boast long-lasting colorful or texture-rich foliage.

Shrubs bring sustained color, form, and height to containers. Choose from flowering or evergreen types and dwarf forms.

Trees are the slowest-growing but longest-lived plant group. Dwarf varieties are especially valuable for their form, bringing height and durability to container gardens.

Vines include sprawling, climbing, and clinging plants, both annual and perennial. They're grown for their form as well as for showy flowers or attractive foliage.

Bulbs, including tubers and bulblike plants, offer splendid flowers or tropical-look foliage for spring, summer, or fall displays.

Tropical plants bring exotic aspects to potted gardens. Many plants grown as annuals are actually tropical or frost-sensitive perennials. Some are commonly sold as houseplants.

Succulents and cactus represent a massive group of plants that are specially adapted to dry, hot climates. Some are cold hardy.

Edibles, such as citrus trees, small fruits, vegetables, and herbs, tantalize senses with their harvestable produce and ornamental aspects. Choose dwarf or compact varieties developed especially for container gardens.

Ornamental assets

When selecting plants, consider their best features: flowers or foliage. Eyecatching flowers grow in an irresistible array of colors and sizes, from the tiny daisies of bacopa to tall willowy angelonia. Foliage also comes in an astounding variety of colors and shapes. Put it to work as a foil for flowers, or grow foliage plants on their own to take advantage of their impressive features. Fantastic containers make use of both flowers and foliage.

Note the plant's growth habit or overall shape. Plants may creep or trail, grow upright, or form a mound. These shapes suggest the best use for the plant in a container.

Be aware of a plant's rate of growth as well as its ultimate size. To ensure a long-lasting composition, only plants with comparable vigor should be grouped in a pot. Otherwise fast growers such as sweet potato will overgrow slower-paced neighbors such as geraniums.

With help from the recipes beginning on page 60, you'll find ways to exploit plants' best attributes in groupings and in single-variety plantings.

opposite In the simplest of garden designs, fern, mandevilla, agave, and bougainvillea create an attractive setting with their singularly striking forms.

above left Take a shortcut to enjoy containers full of spring-flowering bulbs by rounding up presprouted bulbs at a garden center in late winter.

above right Potted edibles make it easy to have on hand your favorite garden-fresh ingredients, such as tomato, dill, purple basil, and kohlrabi.

Designing with Plants

Creating satisfying container schemes requires neither scientific method nor artistic ability. Like guests at a dinner party, some plants have instant rapport. They benefit from the presence of other plants and play off one another's best qualities. Aesthetic strengths balance weaknesses as colors pop and forms mesh harmoniously, enhancing the overall gathering within a compatible container.

Sound like a tall order? It's really quite doable once you begin to recognize the ways in which plants work together to make ideal companions. Whether carefully planned or delightfully spontaneous, the best container schemes come about when you understand a few general design principles. But above all, combine plants and containers to your heart's—and eyes'—content, and then enjoy the effects.

Three main ingredients

Color sets the tone of a garden because you see it first. Warm, bold hues of red, orange, and yellow grab attention with their intensity, even at a distance. Softer pastels and cool blues and purples evoke serenity and have more impact up close. Green and gray harmonize. Experiment with colors and aim for contrasts or at least, complements.

Form is the three-dimensional shape of plants, including their height and spread; it contributes to the garden's overall structure and effect as plants grow. Upright and spiky plants add vertical interest, balancing the plants' height and the garden's overall scale. Midrange fillers (mounded, vase-shape, pyramidal, or arching) add mass and contrast. Trailing plants sprawl and spill over edges, softening the container and anchoring it to its surroundings. A combination of these three forms works dependably well.

Texture adds interest via a plant's foliage and flowers, depending on their size and shape. Wispy or lacy—fine-texture—plants (dahlberg daisy, bacopa, coreopsis) contrast with coarse-texture ones (hydrangea, coleus, Persian shield). Play with a palette of textures from smooth to shiny, velvety, crinkled, and more, and see what happens.

left Foliage interest endures through the seasons, especially in groups. Here, ornamental grasses (*Miscanthus* and fountain grass) team with *Melianthus,* aloe, woolly thyme, echeveria, and coleus, among others.

top Containers of colorful plants, such as the hibiscus, coleus, and New Guinea impatiens in the foreground, will help you create places to relax and enjoy the surroundings.

above It takes only a few minutes to replace plants in a container, adding the fresh color of primroses, for example, or adjusting a less-than-pleasing design.

above As plants grow, their relationships within a container change, so base your selections on their potential size at maturity. You'll find the details on a plant's tag.
opposite Buy bedding plants by the flat and get a quantity discount.

Buying Plants

Make sure your container gardens get the best start possible by choosing healthy plants that are well suited to your location. Many nontraditional retailers, such as groceries, hardware stores, and mass merchants, offer plants seasonally, so it pays to be on your toes when shopping. Try to buy the same day that plant shipments arrive at the store. Freshly shipped from a nursery, plants are usually in good shape and may not have had time to suffer from inadequate care.

Reliable, dedicated garden centers are set up for long-term care of plants. They offer a selection of organized, well-labeled, vigorous plants and a knowledgeable staff who are able to answer questions. Perennial and woody plants often come with a guarantee, unless they're end-of-the-season clearance stock. Whether you shop at garden centers, nurseries, greenhouses, or nontraditional outlets, knowing what to look for makes the process more enjoyable.

Keep tabs on tags

Surprisingly, stores often sell plants that are not right for their region. Hardiness, care information, and other details, such as a plant's potential size and need for light and water, can be found on plant tags. Read and save tags for future reference.

Choose for health

Scrutinize plants from top to bottom. Look for strong, evenly colored stems and foliage, lots of flower buds, and a web of mostly pale roots in a mass with soil. (Gently remove the pot to check the roots.) Use these clues to avoid buying problems:
Wilted or discolored foliage may indicate faulty watering, sun- or cold-related injury, nutrient deficiency, or disease.
Tightly wound root balls without soil indicate a rootbound, undesirable plant.
Straggly stems and lots of spent flowers may indicate the end of a plant's bloom season, neglect, inadequate light, or damage due to pests or disease.

BHG
CONTAINER
BASICS

BE A WISE SHOPPER Plants are sold in a confusing range of sizes, containers, and prices. Before you buy, think about which is the better deal: smaller, cheaper plants or larger, pricier ones? It depends. When you spend more for a larger plant, you get the immediate impact that it takes several weeks to get with smaller plants. Filling numerous large containers this way is costly, however, and smaller plants in 4- or 6-packs will provide plenty of flower power over the course of a season for less money.

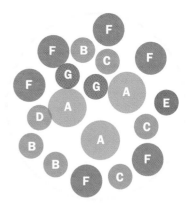

Essentials
Container: 18-inch glazed pot
Light: Sun
Water: Keep soil damp; use drip irrigation to ensure consistent moisture daily

Ingredients
A. 3 geranium ('Crystal Palace Gem')
B. 3 orange-and-bronze pansy
C. 3 purple pansy
D. 1 marigold
E. 1 red verbena
F. 6 swan river daisy
G. 2 chartreuse licorice plant

Notes
Bright blossoms abound in this all-annual scheme, but the geraniums' lime green foliage glows. Packing the plants shoulder to shoulder in the container contributes to its immediate success. Six-month time-release fertilizer granules mixed into the soil at planting help sustain the show throughout summer.

BASICS

BABY PLANTS
Annuals are widely available as young plants in multiple-cell nursery packs. Buying annuals in cell packs is economical, but the plants have little room for rooting and will require close attention to watering, feeding, and deadheading. Plant young annuals as soon as possible with space to spread their roots and grow.

Annual Spectacular

Brightly colored annuals put on a glorious season-long show. The vibrant colors come from a mix of flowers and foliage that forms a grand bouquet. The choice of colors depends on your preference for bold or subtle, with variety as the key.

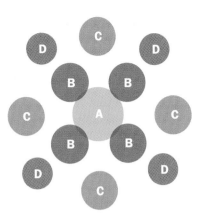

Essentials

Container: 18-inch ceramic pot
Light: Sun
Water: Let soil begin to dry between waterings

Ingredients

A. 1 porcupinegrass *(Miscanthus sinensis* 'Strictus')
B. 4 celosia ('Fresh Look Yellow')
C. 4 variegated lemon thyme *(Thymus citriodorus* 'Variegata')
D. 4 moneywort ('Goldilocks')

Notes

Easy on the eye, a green-on-green garden creates a refreshing effect that calms and soothes. Choosing variegated plants, splashed with yellow or striated with white, brightens the overall effect. Full-sun exposure enhances variegation in most plants. For a similar effect in a shadier site, look for variegated shade lovers such as sedge, Swedish ivy, and English ivy.

FUN IN THE SUN

Full sun = at least six hours of direct sun daily.
Part sun = at least three to six hours of sun daily. Also called part shade or light shade, this term describes sites that receive filtered or dappled light all day.

SUN

Hues of Green

A single-color, or monochromatic, container design allows you to master the brushstrokes of form and texture. When all-foliage plants in a container are a similar color, it's the contrast between their shapes, sizes, and textures that makes each plant more prominent. The overall result: a composition that sparkles.

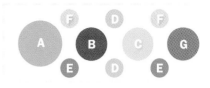

Essentials
Container: 25-inch-long lightweight polystyrene planter
Light: Sun
Water: Water daily to keep soil damp

Ingredients
A. 1 rose-scented geranium
B. 1 apricot-pink giant hyssop (*Agastache rupestris*)
C. 1 white Texas sage (*Salvia coccinea* 'Alba')
D. 2 yellow nasturtium
E. 2 white lantana
F. 2 white globe amaranth (*Gomphrena globosa*)
G. 1 variegated Swedish ivy

Notes
Several of the plants included in this container have ornamental value only. The lantana, globe amaranth, and Swedish ivy are NOT edible, while the hyssop, nasturtium, and scented geranium are edible. Scented geraniums, available in an amazing selection from citrusy to spicy, minty, and fruity, also enhance plantings with their varied leaf shapes and sizes.

FRAGRANT PLANTS
Potent perfumes distinguish many flowers, but did you know that many plants pack pleasant aromas in their leaves instead? Most herbs are known for their scented foliage in addition to their flavors and ornamental properties.

Boxed Delights

Scented leaves and edible flowers pack a planter with all-summer pleasures. Planning a container according to a theme simplifies the process and rewards your creativity.

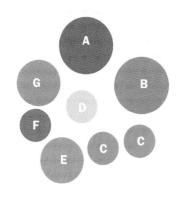

Essentials

Container: 24-inch wooden tub
Light: Sun
Water: Keep soil barely damp

Ingredients

A. 1 trumpet honeysuckle
(Lonicera sempervirens)
B. 1 coral autumn sage
C. 2 Japanese sedge
D. 1 licorice plant
E. 1 hybrid fuchsia
F. 1 yellow-and-red lantana
G. 1 salmon canna with purple
foliage *(Canna x generalis* 'Philip')

Notes

Red, orange, and bright pink
flowers attract hummingbirds;
trumpet- and tubular-shape
blossoms have the most nectar-
promising appeal. Early- and
late-season bloomers flag down
hummers as they migrate.

BIG CAN-DO DESIGN

VIEWING STATION

Place the Hummer Haven within
view of your patio, deck, or porch
where you can watch winged
traffic while you relax. As the birds
flit in and out of the garden to
gather nectar, they also snag tiny
insects essential to their diet.

SUN

Hummer Haven

Hummingbirds have magical charm, with wings
that beat up to 78 times per second and a long
bill that enables them to sip flowery nectar.
Set up this container garden to welcome these
reliable pollinators to your deck or patio and
reward them with a sweet feast.

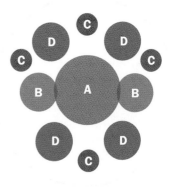

Essentials

Container: 20-inch terra-cotta pot
Light: Sun
Water: Daily watering helps maintain evenly moist soil

Ingredients

A. 1 Chinese hibiscus
B. 2 Japanese blood grass (*Imperata cylindrica* 'Rubra')
C. 4 red scarlet sage
D. 4 red New Guinea hybrid impatiens

Notes

Chinese hibiscus is the star of this garden. You can train hibiscus into a standard, but it's faster and easier to start with a ready-made one. Encourage summer-long bloom by pinching spent flowers and fertilizing monthly. In cold climates overwinter the hibiscus indoors in a cool, sunny spot, removing the other plants before bringing it in. Care for it as you do your other houseplants.

BIG CONTAINER BASICS

THE WAY TO STARDOM

When combining plants in a container, it helps to establish a focal point that draws the eye and gives it a place to rest. The focal point, or star plant, creates an orderly yet dramatic effect in the design. Choose one that shines for its height, color, form, or other outstanding feature.

Red Hot & Sassy

This fiery grouping of red blossoms will raise your spirits. As a bonus, the color of the nectar-rich flowers attracts butterflies and hummingbirds all summer. Red-tipped Japanese blood grass unites the upper and lower tiers of bloom while adding interest to the planting.

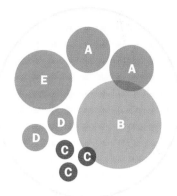

Essentials

Container: 22-inch wine or whiskey half barrel
Light: Sun
Water: When the soil begins to feel dry

Ingredients

A. 2 canna ('Tropicanna')
B. 1 firebush (*Hamelia patens*)
C. 3 orange narrow-leaf zinnia
D. 2 yellow lantana
E. 1 purple fountain grass

Notes

Enriching standard potting soil with compost and rotted manure helps keep large plants growing strong all summer. Fertilize monthly. At the end of the season, dig up the canna rhizomes and store them in a cool dry spot for next year's garden.

BIG CONTAINER BASICS

TALL TALES

Large tropical-looking accent plants draw attention to a mixed container with their height, oversize colorful foliage, and dramatic effect. You can lend stature to any container with architectural plants such as tall cannas, angel's trumpet (*Brugmansia* spp.), 'Tiger Eyes' sumac (*Rhus typhina* 'Bailtiger'), elephant's ear, or banana (*Musa* spp.).

SUN

Drama Queen

To create drama with a potted garden, think BIG as you plan. Scale makes the difference. Start with a container large enough to sustain plants that say, "Look at me!" This garden's overall size and color and the motion of the ornamental grass enable it to compete in a similarly dramatic location next to a waterfall.

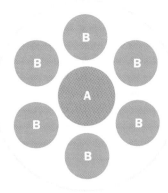

Vine Lines

Pair fast-growing morning glory and hop vines with a simple support to make a colorful and dramatic plant tower. Who would guess the support structure consists of tomato cages held in place with coat hangers?

Essentials

Container: 24-inch terra-cotta pot
Light: Sun
Materials: two large five-hoop tomato cages; two wire coat hangers; 20-gauge wire
Water: Daily watering helps maintain evenly moist soil

Ingredients

A. 1 golden hops (*Humulus lupulus* 'Aureus')
B. 6 morning glory (*Ipomoea tricolor*)

Notes

Morning glory vines start easily from seed but have a hard seed coat that can slow germination. To promote sprouting, scuff the seeds between two sheets of sandpaper to nick their coats, then soak the seeds in water overnight. Sow them in a 3- to 4-inch pot the next day.

PLANT SWAP

ALTERNATIVE PLANTINGS

Substitute vining duos:
• Virginia creeper (*Parthenocissus quinquefolia*) and maypop (*Passiflora incarnata*)
• Malabar spinach and scarlet runner bean
• Jasmine and canary creeper (*Tropaeolum peregrinum*)

step 1

step 2

HERE'S HOW...

1 Prepare the pot

Bend the coat hangers and place them in the pot's bottom with the hooks on opposite sides near the rim. Fill the container with potting mix to just below the hooks.

2 Place the center plant

Center the hops in the container. Stack the tomato cages, shifting one so the cages' legs alternate and form a grid for the vines to climb. Set the cages upside down on the potting mix surface. Hook the hangers over the bottom rungs, pinching them closed with pliers to hold the cages in place.

3 Finish planting

Plant morning glory seedlings around the edge of the container. Cover all root balls with potting mix. Cinch the legs of the tomato cages together by wrapping wire around them. Bend the ends of the legs with pliers to form hooks and create a decorative finish to the tower.

step 3

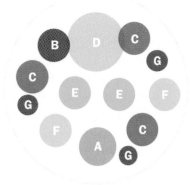

Essentials

Container: 18-inch yellow glazed ceramic pot
Light: Sun
Water: As needed to keep soil consistently damp

Ingredients

A. 1 golden oregano (*Origanum vulgare* 'Aureum')
B. 1 green-and-white coleus ('Wizard Jade')
C. 3 white-speckled-green coleus ('Emerald & Snow')
D. 1 porcupinegrass (*Miscanthus sinensis* 'Strictus')
E. 2 marigold ('Sweet Cream')
F. 2 pale yellow petunia
G. 3 variegated vinca

Notes

Wait until the weather has warmed at night to plant this mix of warm-season annuals (coleus, marigold, petunia, vinca) and perennials. At the end of the season, you can transplant the perennials—porcupinegrass and golden oregano—into your garden to return the following spring.

BHG TEST GARDEN TIP

COLEUS FOR SUN; COLEUS FOR SHADE

Traditionally grown for its brilliant foliage in shade, coleus comes in a kaleidoscope of colors as well as leaf shapes and sizes. Many of the newer varieties on the market have been bred for sun and grow marvelously in sun or shade.

Lemon-Lime Punch

Pick yellow and green to create a simple-as-can-be plant combination with a harmonious and energetic effect. This garden works well with almost any house color because green—the dominant hue—is a neutral color. Green also adds contrast and brightness.

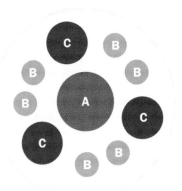

Essentials

Container: 18-inch blue-purple glazed ceramic pot
Light: Sun
Water: When soil begins to feel dry

Ingredients

A. 1 red copperleaf
(*Acalypha wilkesiana*)
B. 6 pink petunia
C. 3 sweet potato ('Blackie')

Notes

As a fast-growing plant, ornamental sweet potato can quickly take over and dominate a mixed planting. Group it with comparable growers or control its rambunctiousness by whacking it back from time to time.

EASY THREESIES

Solve the mystery of choosing plants for containers with this popular formula: Pick a thriller, an upright plant, for vertical structure. Add a filler, a bushy plant, for balance. Mix in a spiller, a cascading plant, to edge the pot and anchor the grouping. Each plant type works with the others to create a balanced design, even when there's only one of each.

Three's a Charm

Take a cue from garden designers: In terms of planting strategies, three is not a crowd but a dependable approach to making effective plant combinations. Using plants in odd numbers like three results in well-balanced, pleasing arrangements.

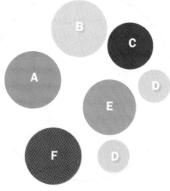

Essentials

Container: 18-inch metallic green glazed pot
Materials: 24-inch-tall black powder-coated wire trellis
Light: Sun
Water: Keep soil damp

Ingredients

A. 1 silver sage (*Salvia argentea*)
B. 1 white cypress vine (*Ipomoea quamoclit* 'Alba')
C. 1 ornamental pepper ('Black Pearl')
D. 2 white double trailing petunia
E. 1 flowering kale ('Chidori White')
F. 1 reflexed stonecrop (*Sedum rupestre* 'Angelina')

Notes

Notice how the planting scheme starts low, at the left edge of the pot, then spirals up to the right, progressing with taller plants and a cypress vine climbing the trellis. Although plants blend with one another in unexpected ways, you'll enjoy more successful container gardens if you plan with the plants' ultimate size in mind.

CAN-DO DESIGN

INSTANT HARMONY

This garden takes a no-fail approach to garden design, moving one step beyond a monochromatic (one-color) scheme. It mixes hues of green and silvery green foliage with white flowers for a soft effect.

Subtle & Soothing

One of the easiest and most effective ways to achieve elegance in garden design comes by combining green and white. Green-dominant container gardens work best when displayed in contrast with a light-color wall, fence, or other background.

Essentials
Container: Five 12- to 16-inch terra-cotta pots
Light: Sun
Water: Keep soil evenly moist

Ingredients
A. 1 licorice plant
B. 1 marguerite daisy ('Butterfly')
C. 1 hollyhock mallow
D. 1 verbena ('Babylon Deep Pink')
E. 1 angelonia ('Serena Purple')

Notes
Angelonia stands among the ranks of newer long-blooming annuals bred to cope with the hot, humid weather that comes with summer. It's also a long-lasting cut flower. No wonder it's sometimes called summer snapdragon. When flower stems become bare and lanky, cut them off at their base.

CONTAINER BASICS

LONE STARS
Grouping single-plant pots near an entryway makes it convenient to trade out plants whenever you want. Add a seasonal beauty that you found at a plant sale. Move one container to the garden, replacing it with a summering houseplant. Swap a couple of containers just to shake things up. Whatever your motivation, growing single plants in single pots makes flexibility possible.

Singles Only

Take the easiest approach possible when it comes to combining plants: Create a composition with a group of pots rather than combining plants in one pot. This technique is most effective when the containers share a similarity. In this case, each terra-cotta pot holds a single, distinctive plant.

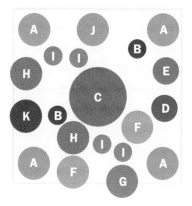

Essentials

Container: 19-inch-square wooden box, lined with sheet plastic; drainage holes cut in both
Light: Sun
Water: Keep soil damp

Ingredients

A. 2 yellow and
2 orange nasturtium
B. 2 russet-orange French marigold
C. 1 red miniature rose
D. 1 grape tomato
E. 1 parsley (Petroselinum crispum)
F. 2 cottage pink
(Dianthus plumarius)
G. 1 sweet potato ('Margarita')
H. 2 mint (Mentha spp.)
I. 4 yellow-and-purple johnny-jump-up
J. 1 dill (Anethum graveolens)
K. 1 common sage ('Tricolor')

Notes

Not all flowers are edible. But many more than those shown here are available and fun to eat, including pansy, daylily, and the blossoms of most herbs. Snip edible flowers and herbs often to keep plants lush and providing tasty harvests all summer.

BHG TEST GARDEN TIP

YOU ARE WHAT YOU EAT
Serve only flowers that you have grown without using toxic herbicides and pesticides.

Tasty Treats

This garden supplies you with fresh, delectable blossoms that add colorful gourmet confetti to food. Edible flowers are best eaten by the petal—rather than whole—so you can savor their typically delicate flavors.

Essentials

Container: 1 each, 15×24-, 20×32-, and 23×40-inch lightweight pots
Light: Sun
Water: When soil begins to feel dry

Ingredients

A: 'Jewel Mix' nasturtium, 'Sweet'n Early' cantaloupe, and 'Porto Rico' bush sweet potato
B: tomato ('Health Kick' and 'Patio Princess'), sweet pepper ('Red Delicious'), and hot pepper ('Mariachi')
C: kale ('Dwarf Blue Curled Vates' and 'Red Winter'), Italian parsley, basil ('Summerlong'), oregano, and marjoram
D: basil and Italian parsley

Notes

Blueberries, strawberries, carrots, and kale are among the most antioxidant-rich foods you can grow. There's a correlation between the deeper, brighter color of produce and its health-enhancing benefits.

SMALL IS BEAUTIFUL

To find varieties of edibles that are best suited to growing in containers, look for names or descriptions of plants that include the words dwarf, compact, pixie, or patio. Such varieties are specifically bred for small-space gardens.

Goodness Grows

Get a bumper crop of heart-healthy nutrition from extra-large pots of vegetables, herbs, and fruits. The crops supply an array of antioxidants, or powerful disease-fighting compounds, for your everyday meals.

Essentials

Container: 4-foot-long window box
Light: Sun
Water: When soil begins to feel dry

Ingredients

A. 4 yellow lantana
B. 5 purple (annual) verbena
C. 2 white pentas
D. 4 creeping zinnia (*Sanvitalia speciosa*)
E. 3 purple globe amaranth (*Gomphrena globosa*)
F. 4 zinnia ('Profusion White')
G. 5 yellow French marigold
H. 3 rose purple calibrachoa
I. 3 pink-flowering white gaura
J. 7 curly parsley

Notes

Provide plants that serve all of butterflies' life stages. They need places to lay eggs and form a chrysalis; leaves, stems, and buds for caterpillars to feed on; and nectar for adults. Red, yellow, orange, pink, or purple flowers tend to attract the most adult butterflies. Parsley, carrot, dill, fennel, and nasturtium are favorites of caterpillars, depending on the butterflies common in your area.

TEST GARDEN TIP

GREENER GARDENS

Refrain from using toxic pesticides and herbicides near your Butterfly Banquet. They're lethal to butterflies as well as bees, lady beetles, and other beneficial insects.

Butterfly Banquet

Turn the space outside your window into an irresistible stop for nature's brightly colored winged beauties by offering their favorite foods in a collection of easy-care flowering plants.

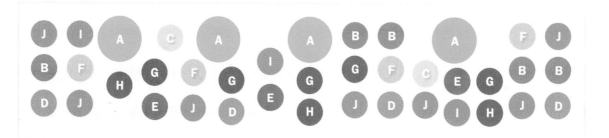

Use any extra plants in cell packs to fill in between bigger plants.

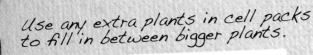

step 1

step 2

HERE'S HOW...

1 Prepare the window box

Use a plastic liner to help preserve the integrity of a wooden window box. Set the potted plants in the liner to determine a pleasing arrangement: Place taller plants in back; drape arching plants over edges.

2 Fill the liner with potting mix

Unpot the plants and nestle their root balls into the potting mix. Cover the root balls with potting mix, leaving an inch of space below the box's rim to allow for watering.

3 Help plants get off to a good start

Spread ½ inch of mulch (shredded bark or cocoa shells) over the soil. Water thoroughly, until water begins to drip from the container's bottom. From then on, water when the soil begins to feel dry.

Water well; pinch spent flowers to encourage growth.

step 3

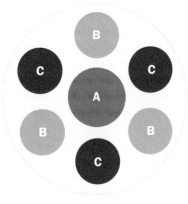

Essentials

Container: 30-inch clay pot
Light: Sun
Water: Keep soil moist

Ingredients

A. 1 Abyssinian red banana
(*Ensete ventricosum* 'Maurelii')
B. 3 plectranthus ('Silver Shield')
C. 3 geranium ('Crystal
Palace Gem')

Notes

Besides ornamental bananas,
you'll find a wealth of large,
exotic-looking plants that
grow easily in containers.
Consider these: bougainvillea,
bird-of-paradise (*Strelitzia
reginae*), ti plant (*Cordyline
fruticosa*), Chinese hibiscus,
and sago palm (*Cycas revoluta*).

DID YOU KNOW?

TOP BANANA

Abyssinian red banana is prized
for its stunning red-tinged
foliage. Confined to a container,
it reaches 6 to 10 feet tall in one
summer. The plant prefers part
shade in a hot climate, but full
sun brings out the deepest
red coloration. Protect it from
frost and bring indoors over
winter in Zones 8 and colder.

Bodacious Banana

Ornamental bananas grow well in containers,
delivering a tropical punch to a roomy patio
or deck with their massive size, umbrella-like
leaves, and exotic silhouettes.

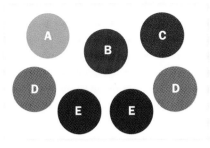

Essentials

Container: 12×15×10-inch vintage bread box
Light: Sun
Water: When soil begins to feel dry

Ingredients

A. 1 yellow chard
B. 1 basil ('Purple Ruffles')
C. 1 ruby chard
D. 2 oregano ('Aureum')
E. 2 chile peppers

Notes

Instead of punching a drainage hole in a metal breadbox or comparable vintage container, place a 3-inch layer of foam packing peanuts in the bottom of it to accommodate runoff from watering. The container may rust or corrode.

SEED MONEY

It makes cents to grow your favorite greens, veggies, and edible flowers from seed. Get a head start on your garden by planting seeds indoors in late winter or early spring. Transplant seedlings into containers outdoors after any threat of frost has passed.

Beauty of the Bounty

What's big as a bread box and provides easy, delicious pickings? This portable kitchen garden proves you don't need a large plot to raise sun-ripened produce.

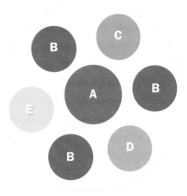

Essentials

Container: 14-inch earthenware pot with a rough exterior texture
Light: Sun
Water: Allow soil to dry a bit between waterings

Ingredients

A. 1 dwarf purple fountain grass ('Red Riding Hood')
B. 3 fiber-optic grass (*Isolepis cernua* 'Live Wire')
C. 1 *Ptilotus exaltatus* 'Joey'
D. 1 dittany of Crete (*Origanum dictamnus*)
E. 1 white strawflower (*Bracteantha bracteata* 'Dreamtime')

Notes

Ornamental grasses and sedges are a wonderful way to add unusual texture, movement, and long-season character to a plant combination. The purple grass and fiber-optic grass (actually a sedge) in this garden grow quickly.

CONTAINER BASICS

TOUCHABLE TEXTURES

The allure of textural foliage and flowers is delightfully irresistible. Take advantage of dittany of Crete's softly felted leaves and let *Ptilotus* tickle you by placing this garden where it can be easily seen and touched, such as near a bench or walkway.

Touchy-feely Garden

This garden gets its "touch me" appeal from its textural residents, including delicate grass and sedge, velvety foliage, and crunchy strawflowers. The plants' drought tolerance also gives the combination the convenience of low maintenance.

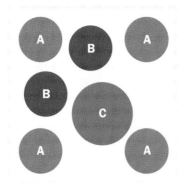

Essentials
Container: 14-inch-square galvanized box
Light: Sun
Water: Keep soil damp

Ingredients
A. 4 variegated sedge ('Evergold')
B. 2 aster ('Purple Dome')
C. 1 ornamental kale ('Nagoya')

Notes
Many colorful annuals thrive in cool fall weather and even shake off frost. Use these generously in your autumn containers: marguerite daisy, ornamental cabbage, twinspur (*Diascia* hybrids), dusty miller, African daisy, pansy, sweet alyssum, snapdragon, stock (*Matthiola incana*), and chrysanthemum.

INSTANT IMPACT
Instantly achieve pleasing results by filling a container with mature plants. Large, fully blooming plants look well established. The most colorful ones provide maximum decorative effect. When shopping, avoid annuals that have reached their peak and will soon set seed and fade.

SUN

Fall Fireworks

Visit a local garden center in late summer or early fall to round up some cool-season plants. Tuck a few brightly colored selections into an unusual container just for fun, or freshen existing displays by replacing tired-looking summer annuals with fall bloomers.

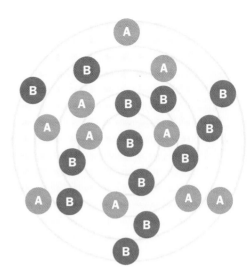

Essentials

Container: 1 each, 6-, 8-, 10-, 12-, and 14-inch pots
Materials: ½-inch wood dowel, 36 inches long
Light: Sun to part shade
Water: Keep soil moist; water daily during hot weather

Ingredients

For one tower of five pots:
A. 10 hot pink calibrachoa
B. 13 purple calibrachoa

Notes

The wooden dowel helps stabilize the tower. If the tower will sit on the ground, drive the dowel into the earth below for greater stability. Vary the garden's effect using calibrachoa of other colors—imagine yellow and lavender—or substitute petunias. If you wish to grow your tower in a shady spot, plant impatiens instead.

BHG TEST GARDEN TIP

KEEP FLOWERS COMING

Use a slow-release liquid fertilizer weekly when you water to keep the plants blooming and growing all season. If plants begin to grow spindly by late summer, cut them back by one-third to encourage new, lush growth.

Blooming High-rise

This tower of terra-cotta pots resolves a small-space challenge and uses the colorful blooms of cascading calibrachoa, a petunia cousin, to make an entryway more welcoming. The winsome effect continues from spring through fall.

Gather the materials where you plan to grow the tower.

step 1

step 2

HERE'S HOW...

1 Position the bottom pot first

Gather materials and build the high-rise in place. Fill the largest pot with potting mix. Push the dowel through the potting mix, centering it over the drain hole.

2 Stack smaller pots by size

Slide the next-smaller pot over the dowel and set it on top of the soil in the pot beneath it. Fill the second pot with potting mix. Repeat the steps until the tower is complete.

3 Set bloomers in place

Plant calibrachoa in the top pot. Tuck plants' root balls into the exposed soil of the remaining pots, alternating colors and leaving 2 to 3 inches between plants.

Water each pot thoroughly. Start at the top so you can wash off any soil that spills over the rim.

step 3

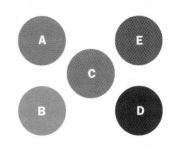

Essentials

Container: 18-inch terra-cotta pot
Light: Sun to part shade
Water: Keep soil damp

Ingredients

A. 1 stevia (*Stevia rebaudiana*)
B. 1 Roman chamomile
(*Chamaemelum nobile*)
C. 1 lemon verbena (*Aloysia triphylla*)
D. 1 pineapple mint (*Mentha suaveolens* 'Variegata')
E. 1 lemon balm
(*Melissa officinalis*)

Notes

Harvest herbs on a sunny morning after the dew has evaporated. For each soothing cup of tea, steep 3 teaspoons of fresh leaves or 1 teaspoon of a dried herb.

CONTAINER BASICS

CREATING THEME GARDENS

Developing a theme for your container gardens makes it easier to organize the plantings, lets you have fun creating extra-special effects, and results in prettier gardens because all the elements relate or are unified. The theme may be inspired by your love for organic tea, a desire to attract wildlife or to celebrate the season, or any other interest you may have.

Tea Time

Grow all the ingredients you need for a cup of freshly brewed herbal tea in this carefree container garden. Fill a container or two with your favorite herbs, such as refreshing mint, calming chamomile, and supersweet stevia. Frequent harvesting keeps plants lush.

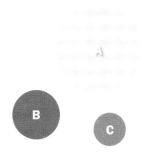

Essentials
Container: 14-inch-square teak planter
Light: Sun to part shade
Water: Keep soil moist

Ingredients
A. 1 hydrangea (Endless Summer)
B. 1 bacopa ('Snowstorm White')
C. 1 moneywort ('Aurea')

Notes
Endless Summer hydrangea is one of a group of *Hydrangea macrophylla* developed for winter hardiness (Zones 4 to 9). Trim off spent flowers to encourage new blooms. In late summer or early fall, transplant the shrub to the landscape.

BUILT TO LAST
When shopping for planters made of teak, look for products made from sustainably grown and harvested lumber. Teak is desirable because it resists moisture, warping, and rot. If you prefer to maintain the teak's original color, apply a wood sealer. Left to weather naturally, the wood will develop a silvery hue.

Easy Elegance

Let a favorite plant such as showy hydrangea set the mood for a container garden. You'll achieve an elegant effect by teaming it with contrasting underplantings and a handsome planter.

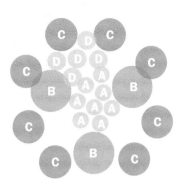

Essentials

Container: 18-inch terra-cotta pot
Light: Part shade to sun
Water: Keep soil damp. Spring rains may handle the job for you.

Ingredients

A. 8 white-and-pink tulip (*Tulipa* 'Diamond')
B. 3 Moroccan toadflax (*Linaria maroccana* 'Fantasy Speckled Pink')
C. 8 pansy ('Panola Pink Shades')
D. 5 white tulip ('Diana')

Notes

Spring-flowering bulbs such as tulips have a brief season of bloom. When the flowers have finished, gently tug the bulbs from the container and replace them with early summer-flowering bulbs such as calla lily.

CONTAINER BASICS

INSTANT SPRING

Most garden centers offer selections of ready-to-grow prechilled bulbs (daffodils, tulips, hyacinths) and cool-season annuals in early spring—perfect for grouping in pots. Buy them in early stages of development, with their green tips barely protruding from the soil, to get the most and longest enjoyment from them.

Rise & Shine

If the gardening season doesn't come soon enough for you, pots of flowers will make your dreams of spring come true in a snap. Welcome early spring with plantings of flowering bulbs and cool-season annuals that can handle the typical temperature swings and light frost of the season.

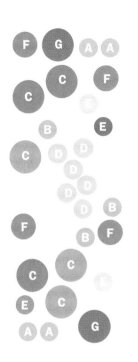

Essentials

Container: 24×15×8-inch lightweight concrete trough
Light: Part shade to sun
Water: Keep soil damp. Spring rains may handle the job for you.

Ingredients

A. 4 yellow tufted California poppy (*Eschscholzia caespitosa*)
B. 3 pink dwarf snapdragon
C. 6 *Felicia heterophylla* (pink; blue) ('Spring Merchen Mix')
D. 6 pink tulip ('Elegant Lady')
E. 4 Persian buttercup (yellow; pink) (*Ranunculus asiaticus* 'Bloomingdale')
F. 4 purple pansy
G. 2 annual candytuft (*Iberis amara*)

Notes

As an alternative, plant a trough with a single variety of prechilled bulbs for big impact. Once the bulbs have finished blooming, toss them on the compost pile and replant the container with summer-flowering annuals.

Mixed Company

This garden's diverse plantings and roomy container create a spring display as pretty as any full-size garden—just the ticket for lifting spirits from late-winter doldrums. Include plants that may not ordinarily grow in your region such as Persian buttercup, which does best in cool dry-summer climates, and enjoy a blissful out-of-climate experience.

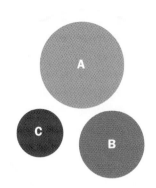

Essentials

Container: 18×24-inch salvaged metal bucket
Light: Shade to part sun
Water: Generously, especially if the container receives sun, to keep soil moist

Ingredients

A. 1 elephant's ear ('Red Stem Rhubarb')
B. 1 coleus ('Sedona')
C. 1 sweet potato ('Sweet Caroline Bronze')

Notes

Jump-start elephant's ear indoors in late winter or early spring. Plant the jumbo tuber (bulb) in a pot large enough to contain it, or directly in the bucket, covering the tuber with 2 inches of potting mix. Moisten the mix and move the pot to a warm spot. Once sprouts appear and outdoor weather is above 50°F, move the pot to the garden. Water often enough to keep soil moist throughout the growing season.

PLANT SWAP

ALTERNATIVE PLANTINGS

Stage a comparable show in full sun with 'Pretoria' canna, sun-loving 'Rustic Orange' coleus, and chartreuse licorice plant.

Bold Foliage

Go for the bold with a sure-to-thrill mix of colorful foliage. This daring threesome reaches an exciting height of about 5 feet as it thrills and spills from a nifty old bucket. The show builds on its star performer—a red-stemmed elephant's ear—towering over the planting.

A

A

B

Essentials

Container: 16-inch-square resin and 12-inch ceramic pots
Light: Part shade
Water: When soil begins to feel dry

Ingredients

A. 2 begonia ('Dragon Wing')
B. purple-leaf shamrock (*Oxalis triangularis*) 1 plant or 5 corms

Notes

Move pots of oxalis and begonias in and out of the house as the gardening season comes and goes. Indoors for winter, grow begonias in bright filtered light and provide a source of humidity such as a tray filled with pebbles and water. Oxalis will go dormant on its own; if desired, place it in bright indirect light and water only occasionally while it dies back. Begin watering dormant plants more often in late winter to early spring to spur growth for the new gardening year.

OXALIS BLUFF

Oxalis leaves fold down between sunset and sunrise and during times of extreme drought, heat, or wind. This behavior fools some gardeners into thinking the plant is wilting and needs water, which can lead to overwatering. Always check the soil before watering.

Color in Shade

You'll appreciate begonias and oxalis for their staying power and the color they add to shady spots. Begonias bloom all summer. Oxalis' color comes from its foliage; its dainty pink flowers usually arrive early and last only a few weeks. These easy-to-grow plants are perfect for container gardens because they can remain in their pots indefinitely.

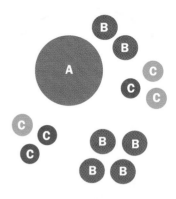

Essentials
Container: 15-inch plastic pot
Light: Part shade
Water: When soil starts to feel dry

Ingredients
A. 1 summer squash (bush type)
B. 6 spinach
C. 6 viola

Notes
A nonporous container minimizes loss of soil moisture. When selecting a pot for your edible garden, look for one made of plastic resin or another nonporous synthetic material that will help you reduce watering frequency. A bright-color container is a bonus for a partly shaded setting.

DID YOU KNOW?

BRIGHT SIDE
Many edible plants, especially ones grown for their leaves or stems (leafy greens or chard), grow well with sun only part of the day. Broccoli, cauliflower, peas, beans, beets, and Brussels sprouts tolerate shade. Plants grown for their fruit or root (tomatoes or potatoes) need full sun to be most productive.

Pot Luck

Given rich, porous soil in a roomy pot and 6 hours or less of sun daily, these edible plants will thrive and taste as good as they look. Harvest the spinach and delicately flavored flowers throughout the spring. Let the squash take over for a summer crop.

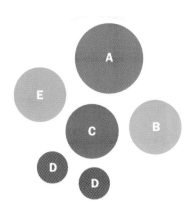

Essentials

Container: 18-inch standard terra-cotta pot
Light: Part shade to sun
Water: Keep soil moist, watering daily during hot weather

Ingredients

A. 1 New Zealand flax
B. 1 geranium ('Happy Thought')
C. 1 elephant's ear ('Black Magic')
D. 2 creeping wire vine
(*Muehlenbeckia axillaris*)
E. 1 giant sword fern (*Nephrolepis biserrata*)

Notes

Each of the plants in this combination, while distinctive, relates to an overall green-purple color scheme. When combining plants—foliage or flowering—in a container, take care to select varieties that have the same needs for sun, shade, water, and fertilizer.

FOLIAGE AS FILLER

Leafy plants work well in container gardens as medium-height, tie-it-all-together elements. A few favorite foliage fillers for a partly shaded spot include perilla, Persian shield, and Japanese painted fern (*Athyrium nipponicum*).

Foliage Finery

A sophisticated combination of green and purple leafy plants draws attention to the edge of a partly shaded deck. The secret to working with foliage is choosing plants in a variety of shapes and sizes, then sitting back and enjoying the nonstop show.

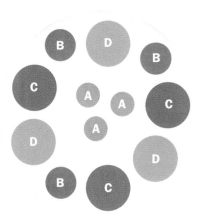

Essentials

Container: 36×48-inch concrete planter
Light: Sun to part shade
Water: Keep soil damp

Ingredients

Core plants

A. 3 ruby grass (*Melinus nerviglumis* 'Pink Champagne')
B. 3 alternanthera ('Purple Knight')
C. 3 chartreuse licorice ('Limelight')
D. 3 heuchera ('Dolce Creme Brûlée')

Spring container (left)

3 purple salvia
6 purple viola
6 purple pansy

Summer container

3 variegated orange-green-white coleus
3 wax begonia 'Cocktail Rum'
3 purple plectranthus

Fall container

3 flowering kale
3 bronze-flowered chrysanthemum ('Blushing Emily')
3 ornamental cabbage

Notes

The seasonal plantings will excel for a time, depending on the weather. When you're ready to change parts of the display, relegate the passé plants to partly shady parts of the garden if you can't bear to compost them.

Seasonal Changeouts

Plant a container garden that goes with the flow, changing with the seasons. Start with a core group of slow-growing, long-lasting foliage plants that will stay put from spring through fall. Combine them with seasonal bloomers, freshening the plantings periodically.

Plant three of each plant, if starting with 4- to 6-inch pots.

step 1

step 2

HERE'S HOW...

1 Change plantings easily

To gently remove a plant without disturbing its neighbors, pry it loose with a trowel or garden fork and tug its root ball free. It helps to slice through the roots first, cutting a circle around the plant with a sharp trowel. Tuck in the new plant and cover its root ball with fresh potting soil.

2 Plant for a summer show

When spring turns to summer, replace cool-season bloomers with heat-tolerant ones. The seasonal availability of plants will affect your scheme. It's likely you'll find lots of options within this purple-peach/orange/pink-chartreuse plant palette.

3 Plant for a fall show

As summer fizzles into fall, pull out spent plants and fill in with cool-season annuals.

Plant multiples of three, if starting with cell packs.

step 3

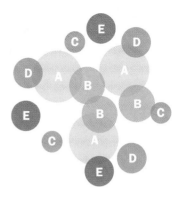

Essentials

Container: 16-inch terra-cotta pot
Light: Part shade to sun
Water: When soil begins to feel dry

Ingredients

A. 3 pink geranium
B. 3 purple nemesia
C. 3 rose pink petunia
D. 3 variegated English ivy
E. 3 green English ivy

Notes

Hundreds of petunias in a myriad of flower colors and plant sizes and habits are available. For container gardening, compact hybrids, such as milliflora and floribunda petunias, offer loads of flowers and tolerate extreme weather well. Nemesia is a cool-weather annual that fades when temperatures rise above the 70s.

BIG CONTAINER BASICS

PINCH AND PLANT

As you plant nursery stock, take a deep breath and pinch off any flowers. Even though you want your container to be in bloom from the start, pinching the flowers prompts plants to direct their energy into rooting, growing bushier, and settling into their new home. In the end, they'll bloom more abundantly too.

Tickled Pink

Harness the energy of annuals for a summerlong show of flower power. Mix old favorites like geraniums with newer varieties such as compact petunias and nemesia in a dependable, sun-loving combination.

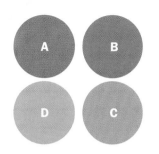

Essentials
Container: 14-inch earthenware pot
Light: Part shade
Water: Keep soil damp

Ingredients
A. 1 Pennsylvania sedge
(Carex pensylvanica)
B. 1 heartleaf skullcap
(Scutellaria ovata)
C. 1 common speedwell
(Veronica officinalis)
D. 1 fringed bleeding heart
(Dicentra exima)

Notes
Many plants dote on the
transitional spaces situated
between fields and woodlands,
partially shaded from the heat of
late-day sun. Choose woodland
plants native to your region.

SUBTLE APPEAL
Far from plain, many native plants
boast impressive, colorful flowers.
Let your native garden be—it will
look good without a lot of bother.

Native Habitat

This pocket-size garden has a wild side: It
brings nature to a small space that doesn't
have access to a natural ecosystem of a field
or woodland. It would be at home on a porch,
sheltered deck, or enclosed patio.

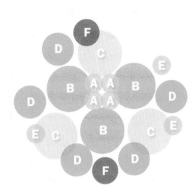

Essentials

Container: 18×19-inch lightweight urn
Light: Part shade
Water: Keep soil damp

Ingredients

A. 4 cosmos ('Sonata')
B. 3 pink-and-white wax or tuberous begonia
C. 3 caladium ('Candidum')
D. 5 yellow archangel (*Lamiastrum galeobdolon* 'Herman's Pride')
E. 3 white mini petunia ('Supertunia')
F. 2 asparagus fern

Notes

Cosmos and petunias require quite a bit of light; at the same time, caladium don't do well in hot sun. Place this garden where it will receive sun from dawn to about noon, and shade for the rest of the afternoon.

BHG CONTAINER BASICS

BENEFITS OF SHADE

Container gardens in shade dry out more slowly and need less watering than ones baking in full sun. However, if your yard is dry and shady, you might prefer to plant in containers because it can be easier to water potted plants and keep the soil more consistently moist than in-ground plantings. What's more, there's a wider array of plants that will grow in moist shade than in dry shade.

Yearning for Shade

White brightens the darkest of corners. Luckily, you can find white in the foliage and flowers of numerous shade plants, including the caladium and yellow archangel in this container garden. Situate the large pot where it can stand out from a green understory.

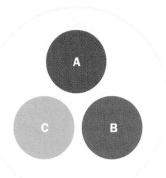

Essentials
Container: 12-inch terra-cotta bowl
Materials: Shells, stones, sea glass, synthetic coral
Light: Part shade
Water: When soil feels dry

Ingredients
A. 1 tufted hairgrass (*Deschampsia caespitosa* 'Northern Lights')
B. 1 little bluestem (*Schizachyrium scoparium* 'Prairie Blues')
C. 1 sedge ('Amazon mist')

Notes
Ornamental grasses, sedges, and other grasslike plants offer the all-season aesthetic benefits of color, texture, and form to your container gardens. Plant them as single specimens or in small groups to show off their best qualities.

BHG PLANT SWAP

COLOR YOUR WORLD
Not all grasses are green! Explore the wealth of small grasses and sedges (less than 12 inches tall) available at nurseries. You'll find a range of foliage hues from blue to coppery brown to orange, as well as variegated types.

Just Beachy
It's easy to create a dunescape that makes the most of a few small ornamental grasses and sedges. Tuck in a handful of seashells and other souvenirs from a seaside vacation. Then display the garden on a table where it can be viewed up close and appreciated.

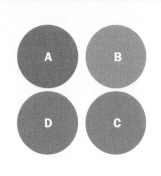

Essentials
Container: 17×11×9-inch basket
Materials: Liner (sheet plastic or moisture-holding type)
Light: Part shade
Water: Keep soil moist

Ingredients
A. 1 peppermint
B. 1 lemon balm (*Melissa officinalis*)
C. 1 spearmint
D. 1 pineapple mint

Notes
Protect the basket from moisture damage by lining it with a sheet of plastic or a moisture-holding material. Poke drainage holes in the plastic at the bottom of the pot. Snip the herbs often to keep them looking lush. If flowers form, pinch them off.

TEST GARDEN TIP

GREGARIOUS MINT
Grow mint plants for the next year from root cuttings taken in fall. When removing the plants from the basket, break off 4-inch pieces of root with a few stems attached. Plant the root sections in a pot and keep the potting mix damp until the stems emerge from the soil. Move the rooted cuttings to bright light, and water when the soil begins to dry.

Contain Your Excite-mint

Keep a basket of mint and lemon balm at hand where you can lean over and snip an aromatic garnish for your drink or harvest some delicious bits to sprinkle on salads or desserts. Mint and the lemony herb are delightfully useful, but they will spread aggressively in garden beds.

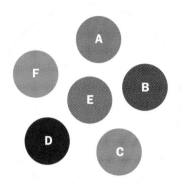

Essentials

Container: 18-inch glazed frostproof pot
Light: Part shade
Water: Keep soil damp. Spring rains may handle the job for you.

Ingredients

A. 1 flowering kale
B. 1 variegated sweet flag *(Acorus gramineus* 'Ogon')
C. 1 alpine wallflower *(Erysium linifolium)*
D. 1 primrose *(Primula auricula* 'Blossom')
E. 1 spurge *(Euphorbia amygdaloides* 'Robbiae')
F. 1 licorice plant *(*'Icicles')

Notes

You can maintain this potted garden year round if your area's climate allows it. (The plants must be two zones hardier than your hardiness zone.) Or if you prefer, transplant the perennials into your garden once the plants have passed their prime. They'll reappear next spring.

WARMER DAYS

If you live in a cold region, wait until nighttime temperatures are consistently above 30°F before planting spring containers. Young plants fresh from the warmth of a greenhouse need to be hardened off—exposed gradually to sun and cool temperatures outdoors.

Spring Fling

Get a head start on the gardening season with a collection of spring's most pleasing cool-weather perennials. Spotlight this container garden by placing it prominently near an entry or along a walkway where everyone passing by can savor its beauty. When the flowers fade, the colorful foliage and mix of textures will keep the planting interesting.

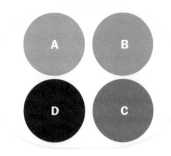

Essentials

Container: 12×6×5-inch oval glazed ceramic pot
Light: Part shade
Water: Keep soil damp

Ingredients

A. 1 nemesia ('Sunsatia Mango')
B. 1 African daisy ('Orange Symphony')
C. 1 heuchera ('Amethyst Mist')
D. 1 spurge (*Euphorbia amygdaloides* 'Efanthia')

Notes

Get the most enjoyment from a fall collection of plants such as this by making it a pretty centerpiece for an outdoor table. Start with well-developed plants in 4-inch pots for instant impact. The heuchera and spurge are hardy perennials that you can move to the garden when the annuals become tired or succumb to frost.

CONTAINER BASICS

EXTEND THE SEASON

Container gardens help you extend the growing season through fall. Fill pots with frost-hardy plants, such as johnny-jump-up, pansy, flowering kale, and dianthus. If your containers include nonhardy plants, cover them at night with an old sheet when temperatures drop below 30°F.

Fall Fashion

Autumn's glory often proves too fleeting. Capture the essence of the season's beauty in a quick and festive display that combines cool-season annuals with bold flowers and colorful perennials with showy foliage.

Essentials

Container: 12-inch galvanized bucket
Light: Part shade or shade
Water: Keep soil damp

Ingredients

A. 1 begonia ('Baby Wing White')
B. 1 lobelia ('Laguna Sky Blue')
C. 1 begonia ('Nonstop Deep Red')

Notes

Unless nearly mature and fully flowering when you buy them, the fastest-growing young annuals take about six weeks to reach their blooming stage. Space plants from cell packs or small (2- to 3-inch) pots about 4 to 6 inches apart, giving them room to fill out.

CONTAINER BASICS

HOLEY BUCKETS

Easily convert a galvanized metal container such as a bucket into a planter by poking at least one hole in its bottom to allow for drainage. Use an awl and hammer to puncture the metal.

Bucket of Blooms

Set off floral fireworks with an explosion of red, white, and blue summer-flowering annuals. Plant by mid-May in order to enjoy fully blooming plants in time for an Independence Day celebration.

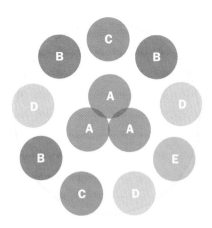

Essentials

Container: 18×24-inch metal urn
Light: Part shade
Water: Keep soil damp

Ingredients

A. 3 angelonia ('Purple Stripe')
B. 3 purple heart ('Purpurea')
C. 2 vinca ('Variegata')
D. 3 verbena ('Lanai')
E. 1 licorice plant ('Lemon Licorice')

Notes

The easy-care plants in this container garden need only water in return for a continual show of color throughout summer. If your plants don't bloom as prolifically as you'd like, move the container to a sunnier spot.

CONTAINER BASICS

PLANT SHOPPING

Choosing plants for a container? Not to worry. As you shop for plants, group them in your shopping cart the way you plan to use them in the container, then step back for a good look. If the grouping appeals to you as much as the individual plants do, you're in business. Be sure the plants you choose have similar needs for light, water, and fertilizer.

Happy Marriage

Arranging plant combinations seems easier if you think of the pot as a vase. Place the main flower in the center, then fill around it with smaller or bushier or trailing flowers. This pretty combo features compatible colors—purple and green—enhanced by white in a sure-to-please arrangement.

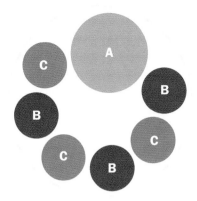

Essentials

Container: 18-inch lightweight polystyrene urn
Light: Shade
Water: Keep soil damp

Ingredients

A. 1 croton (*Codiaeum variegatum pictum*)
B. 3 New Guinea impatiens ('Ovation Red Spice')
C. 3 New Guinea impatiens ('Ovation Suncatcher Orange')

Notes

Move the bold croton or a similarly showy houseplant out of the house and into its summer digs. Before chilly weather returns in fall, move it back indoors.

SHOWER OFF

Houseplants benefit from spending the summer outdoors, where they revel in often-humid conditions and plenty of available light. Before moving them back indoors, give them a forceful shower using the garden hose to chase off any hitchhiking insects.

Color in a Snap

Keep your garden sizzling throughout summer with a red-hot touch of the tropics in a luxurious-looking pot. But this scheme also has economical aspects that will please you the way a budget-conscious vacation would.

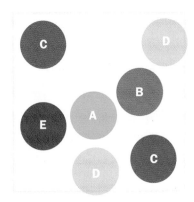

Essentials

Container: 18-inch redwood-stained wooden planter
Light: Part shade
Water: Keep soil damp

Ingredients

A. 1 yellow coleus ('Glennis')
B. 1 New Zealand flax ('Bronze Beauty')
C. 2 bronze coleus ('Sedona')
D. 2 pink trailing verbena ('Aztec Coral')
E. 1 sedge ('Bronzita')

Notes

Coleus has been popular since Victorian times. It's fun to collect numerous varieties and try them with various plant partners to discover your favorite potted combinations. Coleus grows easily; apply fertilizer lightly, if at all.

CAN-DO DESIGN

METAL LEAF

Plant breeders continually work to create new varieties that perform better and meet gardeners' desire to push the envelope with plants. Metallics are one of the latest trends in fashion, home decor, and even gardening. Look for new foliage plants in metallic colors, such as silver, gold, and bronze. They're great for brightening shady corners as well as for being neighborhood trendsetters.

Caramel Eye Candy

Soft colors and an organic-looking container team up, giving this garden casual appeal for a partly shaded brick patio. This planting scheme would work well in a variety of containers, from stone-look resin to terra-cotta, rusted metal, or earthen ceramic.

Essentials

Container: One pot per plant, any style
Light: Part shade
Water: Keep soil moist

Ingredients

A. 1 banana
B. 4 canna
C. 1 kentia palm *(Howea forsteriana)*
D. 1 yellow-and-orange coleus, trained as a standard
E. 1 sky flower *(Duranta erecta)*
F. 1 Chinese hibiscus
G. 2 croton
H. 1 purple fan flower
I. 3 ornamental millet

Notes

If you have plenty of room for a bold display, group large plants in individual pots, clustering multiples of some varieties. You can create a similar effect on a smaller scale by planting smaller selections in one large pot.

CONTAINER BASICS

START A TREND

This container garden turned a stretch of unwelcoming concrete between two urban condos into a meeting place for neighbors. All it takes is for one person to plant a garden for change to begin. Display your container garden where other people can appreciate it. Next thing you know, your neighbors will join in, and soon a community will grow.

Standing Room Only

Grouping pots of single plants in varying sizes, shapes, and heights produces visual impact equal to a large garden bed. This cast of tropical plants can move outdoors as soon as the weather warms but really hits its stride as midsummer cranks up the heat.

CHAPTER FOUR

Places for Plants

Practice strategic planting and put containers to work where they'll provide the most benefits—from the ground up. Use repetition and scale for dramatic effects such as these.

When you have a place in mind for a container garden, you'll do more than add color, shape, and form there. Use potted displays to achieve your landscaping goals, whether you want to enhance privacy, dress up structures, or reach loftier aims. They'll provide opportunities to garden where there is no ground and to overcome the challenges of small spaces.

Anywhere Gardens

Your wish becomes a container garden's command when you have a spot and a purpose in mind for it. Starting at ground level, use containers' versatility to achieve various landscaping goals. Use them, for example, to edge a pathway, screen a sitting area, or frame an entry. Containers' portability enables you to stage them where they will put on the best show or move them elsewhere if need be.

When you look for places to stage containers, consider sites without in-ground growing room. Potted gardens turn decks, patios, and other outdoor spaces into alluring destinations, integrating them with the nearby landscape. Whatever the size of your outdoor area, potted plants provide instant color, form, and interest. Depending on where you place them, containers complement structures and balance hard elements.

Use a single pot to showcase a favorite plant, giving it center stage in a bed, or to fill a gap in the garden where a plant has failed or passed its prime. Mixing plants in a large pot or grouping multiple pots helps paint a garden picture. But the key is not how many pots you have; it's what you do with them.

Positioning containers at your front door highlights the entry, providing a pleasing first impression. Edging a path with pots guides visitors' steps. On stairs, pots bring attention to changes in level and accentuate the architecture. Pots can also define the perimeter of a garden, paved area, or similar landscape element while softening the hard surface. A big-enough potted garden disguises an unsightly view.

Deliberately setting pots here and there can create a sense of movement. Where there's a practical reason for lining up containers—along the perimeter of an outdoor room to boost privacy, for instance—repetition fulfills the task. Pots placed in a row or another pattern strengthen the rhythm for a more pronounced effect.

top Survey your site, then match potted gardens to opportunities. Several pots of lavender, pansies, and petunias step up to colorfully mark an entryway.

above Pots of red dragon wing begonias provide portable spots of color wherever they are most needed from spring into fall.

left A chorus line of potted Madagascar dragontree *(Dracaena marginata)* works well to screen an intimate dining area without blocking the fantastic view.

Raising Your Sights

Take your container gardens to the next level, literally, by raising them off the ground. Elevating a container—anywhere between the ground and eye level—makes it easier to see and appreciate its contents from a distance or within sniffing range. Propped on a plant stand, ledge, wall, or windowsill, a potted garden becomes a showpiece, decorative enough to boost your home's curb appeal. And there's a bonus: When you create plantable areas at more accessible levels, you can garden without crouching or bending—a boon to your back and knees.

Outside the box

Using the vertical dimension helps you make the most of every inch of potential gardening space and make room to garden where there doesn't seem to be any. Window boxes in particular serve many apartment dwellers as the only option for gardening. Where there's a wall, fence, or railing, opportunity exists to parlay available surfaces into space for planting that also makes the structure more appealing.

Take time to explore the array of containers made especially for decks, porches, balconies, and windowsills. Window boxes and lined metal baskets can also be secured to other locations such as porch or deck railings. Use wide, deep planters whenever possible to cover more area with plants. Experiment with cascading plants, including flowering (ivy geraniums and petunias) as well as foliage-only (trailing vinca and plectranthus) options.

The size of usable containers may be limited by their weight when mounted on walls, fences, and railings. Although a steel hayrack lined with coco fiber and filled with ultralight potting mix proves lighter than a large cedar window box, the weight of both increases considerably when saturated with water. Use high-quality containers and building materials; plan to mount containers without taking shortcuts or damaging any structures involved.

above For best results, hang window boxes that are slightly wider than the window frame. Fill them with long-blooming plants such as petunias and fan flower.
left A tiered plant stand offers an easy way to decorate a wall with the seasonal color of pansies and forget-me-nots.
opposite If space is limited, look for ways to grow vertically using cascading plants, such as sweet potato, moneywort, spiderwort, and trailing vinca.

Aiming Higher

Gardeners often overlook vertical space. But container gardens raised to eye level or higher instantly garner attention. When you place favorite plants on a pedestal or choreograph a combination in a high flowering basket, you'll improve the setting and possibly heighten your gardening skills too.

Aerial gardens

Imagine where you might create special interest with a potted garden on a pedestal. An urn serves as a pot with a built-in pedestal. But you can easily fashion a support for almost any pot using a sturdy base such as a concrete block or an overturned pot.

You'll find a new generation of containers similar to hanging baskets but made for mounting on railings, posts, or poles. Freestanding towers with tiered baskets or trellises support trailing plants and provide height anywhere they're needed.

Make the most of hanging plantings (unless they're designed for a wall or fence) by looking for a way to ensure they're visible from all sides. In exchange for the impression made by hanging baskets' voluptuousness, extra maintenance will be needed. The plants in aerial containers often require more watering and feeding because their roots are particularly confined and subject to the drying effects of air circulation. Hang them within reach of convenient watering. Take extra steps to secure any suspended containers. Plenty of sturdy hooks, brackets, and other supports are available to help you handle the job.

On the plus side, aerial containers give you opportunities to incorporate types of plants that expand the use of vertical space. Plants that climb, trail, and cascade are natural acrobats that will enhance your displays. Expanding arrays of petunias, verbenas, ivies, and others are popular for their abilities to tumble and camouflage a hanging basket. Your choice of plants and planting methods can ensure that the container packs a strong visual punch.

right A freestanding container overflowing with Wave petunias, strawflowers, and creeping zinnias adds three-dimensional color to a garden.

below Massive moss-lined baskets, packed with impatiens and other shade-loving plants, provide the most color around a gazebo with the least amount of upkeep.

opposite Fast-growing sweet potato plants spilling out of hanging baskets create a lively privacy screen.

Special Strategies

You don't need a magic wand to become a garden magician. Potted gardens help you expand the potential of any area when you apply visual tricks. Strategically placing containers can lead the eye or distract it, creating an illusion of depth, height, and overall space.

Containers also help you put your gardenable space to good use. You'll gain floor space anytime you raise containers off the ground and use vertical areas to display plantings instead. Wall planters and other hanging containers make it possible to garden in the narrowest spaces (between a house and a fence or between apartment buildings). In addition, you'll minimize the blankness of a wall or fence with containers placed on or near the structure.

Any hanging garden or vertical planting draws the eye upward and extends the feeling of space. On a balcony or porch, for instance, a staged potted garden partially conceals the view and emphasizes a sense of the beyond. Similarly, situating a container on a far wall or in the farthest corner of the patio creates an illusion of depth and increased distance. Employing containers to partition an area into outdoor rooms also gives an impression of size. One way or the other, containers transform a tiny, confined, dull, or otherwise limited space into a lush, interesting garden.

Staging special effects

A deck or patio presents an opportunity for a plant stand, shelving, or similar platform for staging potted plants in space-saving tiers. Combining cool-color plants (especially blues and purples) and pastels strengthens an illusion of depth.

A solitary container enables you to plant a miniature landscape—including a small tree or shrub and colorful underplantings—even in the smallest of spaces. Another way to add height to any container entails outfitting it with a trellis and a climbing plant.

left Placed at various heights, potted gardens flank a path with wax begonias, coleus, and other shade plants, making the walkway more inviting.
below Large concrete bowls planted with turfgrass add seating area to a small patio. Occasional trimming keeps the grass under control.
opposite Cedar window boxes and bright tuberous begonias turn an expanse of gray fence into a wall of blooms.

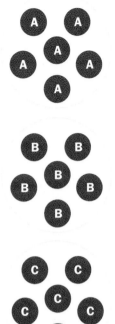

Strawberry Shortstack

Strawberries' shallow roots make them ideal for containers. Keeping plants within easy reach and in a space-efficient planter stacks up to luscious pleasures.

Essentials
Container: 12×36-inch tiered wire basket.
Materials: Landscape fabric or moisture-holding liner and moss
Light: Sun
Water: Keep soil damp

Ingredients
A. 6 strawberry ('Sequoia')
B. 6 strawberry ('Quinault')
C. 6 strawberry ('Ozark Beauty')

Notes
Line each basket to hold in soil and moisture. Plant the crowns (where roots and stems meet) just above soil level. Feed plants every two weeks with a high-phosphorus fertilizer to prompt flowers.

TEST GARDEN TIP

STRAWBERRY YIELDS FOREVER
You'll find varieties of strawberries for different seasons and regions. June-bearing plants offer a short, intense crop in the spring. Everbearing plants produce fruit intermittently from spring into fall. Day-neutral plants fruit throughout the growing season.

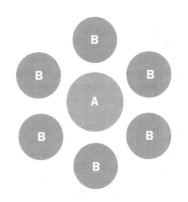

Essentials

Container: 18-inch terra-cotta pot
Light: Sun
Water: Consistent, deep watering when soil begins to feel dry

Ingredients

(for each container)
A. 1 dwarf lemon tree
B. 6 white sweet alyssum

Notes

If you start with a typical two-year-old dwarf tree, choose a 12- to 14-inch container and replant in a larger pot as the tree grows over the years. Protect the tree from freezing. Keep it indoors over winter in cold climates, providing it with 8 to 12 hours of sun daily.

ALTERNATIVE PLANTINGS

'Meyer' is a popular dwarf lemon variety that grows well in a container. Choose from many varieties of other dwarf citrus that are equally well suited to container growing, including: 'Lane Late' navel orange, 'Owari' satsuma mandarin, and 'Bearss' lime.

SUN

First Impressions

A prettily potted dwarf citrus tree—repeated and aligned for impact—benefits from a position near a sun-soaked south-facing wall where it's protected from wind. In any comparable setting, the annual cycle of fragrant blossoms gives way to fresh fruit.

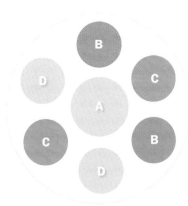

Essentials

Container: 19×22-inch fiberglass urn
Light: Sun
Water: When the soil begins to feel dry

Ingredients
(for each container)

A. 1 rose ('Iceberg')
B. 2 English ivy ('Glacier')
C. 2 catmint ('Walker's Low')
D. 2 white bacopa

Notes

'Iceberg' is a long-blooming, practically thorn-free rose. Sustain its flower show by providing monthly doses of rose food and regularly snipping off spent blooms.

CONTAINER BASICS

THE BIG PICTURE

One way to achieve success with large compositions such as this entails letting the main or accent plant claim one-third of the display with supporting players and the container taking the other two-thirds.

Worth Repeating

Maximize a container's effect by starting with a large pot and a stellar plant. Heighten the starring plant's performance with a supporting cast of complementary trailing plants. Then repeat the drama in duplicate displays as much as space allows.

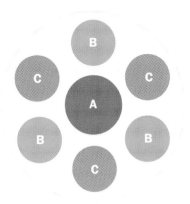

Essentials

Container: 16×16-inch fiberglass urn; 18×18-inch square pot for pedestal
Light: Sun
Water: Keep soil on the dry side

Ingredients

(for each container)

A. 1 dwarf century plant (*Agave desmettiana*)
B. 3 ice plant (*Lampranthus deltoides*)
C. 3 reflexed stonecrop (*Sedum rupestre* 'Angelina')

Notes

Match containers by applying a faux finish, if necessary. Use a potting mix of one-third each soilless potting mix, sand, and perlite.

BHG CAN-DO DESIGN

SUCCULENT ACCENTS

When choosing containers for succulents, pay attention to the overall look of the pot and the plants, aiming to highlight both elements. A vertical agave shines in a vertical pot that accentuates its shapeliness, for instance.

SUN

Living Sculptures

Play up the artful qualities of succulents by displaying them simply. Place your potted garden on overturned pots to grab attention with the bold forms of the plants as well as the containers.

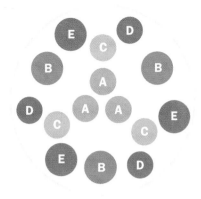

Essentials

Container: 18-inch terra-cotta pot
Light: Sun
Water: Keep soil damp

Ingredients

A. 3 pink snapdragon
B. 3 pink petunia
C. 3 pink wax begonia
D. 3 purple petunia
E. 3 English ivy

Notes

Choose annuals that repeat the color theme of nearby gardens to create a unified look.

BHG
TEST
GARDEN
TIP

COMMAND PERFORMANCES

Take advantage of the repetitive blooming behavior of some annual plants known as cut-and-come-again flowers. The more you cut the flowers for a vase, the more the plants will bloom. Try snapdragon, zinnia, cosmos, gaillardia, and salvia.

Summer Hospitality

Take a relaxed approach to your container designs. They'll reward you by setting a casual tone wherever you place them. An armload of bedding plants plus a couple of stalwarts such as ivy will surely make a cheerful statement.

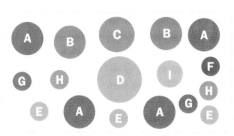

Essentials
Container: 48-inch window box
Light: Sun
Water: When soil begins to feel dry

Ingredients
A. 4 Italian flat-leaf parsley
B. 2 basil
C. 1 marjoram
D. 1 lemon thyme
E. 3 mint
F. 1 cilantro
G. 2 viola
H. 2 marigold
I. 1 thyme

Notes
Harvest a small bouquet of herbs
and keep it handy in a vase of
water on the kitchen counter.

BETTER FLAVOR
Eat your herbs, but don't feed
them! Herbs do not require
fertilizer to grow well. What's
more, feeding promotes growth
at the expense of flavor.

SUN

In Good Taste
The best-dressed windows include a garden.
And a window box with a sunny view presents
the perfect place to keep summer herbs and
edible flowers within snipping range.

Long-term Lease

A massive window box pumps up a home's curb appeal by adding charm with a succulent and evergreen twist. The best window boxes can be viewed and admired from the street.

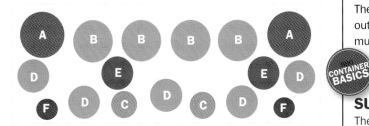

Essentials

Container: 6-foot-long cedar window box
Light: Part shade or sun
Water: Keep soil on the dry side

Ingredients

A. 2 upright juniper
B. 4 agave
C. 2 burro's tail (*Sedum morganianum*)
D. 5 ghost plant (*Graptopetalum paraguayense*)
E. 2 giant echeveria
F. 2 stonecrop (creeping variety)

Notes

The hardiness of succulent plants varies. Some can remain outdoors year round in Zones 7 and warmer areas. Many must spend winter indoors in order to survive.

BHG
CONTAINER
BASICS

SUCCULENT FACTS

These plants have evolved to withstand periods of little or no rain by storing water in their fleshy leaves or bulbous roots. If you water succulents too much, the plants will rot.

SUN

High & Mighty

Beautify a deck railing, fence, or other structure easily with a potted garden. This rectangular planter straddles the railing—no hardware required—and employs the plants' cascading talents to form a verdant curtain.

Essentials

Container: 14×12×8-inch plastic deck-rail planter
Light: Sun
Water: When soil begins to feel dry

Ingredients

A. 2 trailing vinca ('High Color')

B. 2 dichondra ('Silver Falls')

C. 1 dark rose angelonia ('Angel Mist')

D. 1 white phlox (Intensia)

E. 2 archangel (*Lamiastrum galeobdolon* 'Jade Frost')

F. 2 verbena (Superbena Pink Parfait)

G. 1 variegated Swedish ivy

Notes

Let trailing or vining plants fill vertical space with their foliage and flowers, especially where there is little room for a garden. Place trailing plants at the container's edge for the best effects.

ALTERNATIVE PLANTINGS

Try these cascading or trailing options: Calibrachoa, Tahitian bridal veil *(Tradescantia multiflora),* fuchsia, and trailing snapdragon. Vines could include sweet potato, black-eyed susan vine, hyacinth bean, and scarlet runner bean.

(E) (F) (G) (F) (E)

(A) (B) (C) (D) (B) (A)

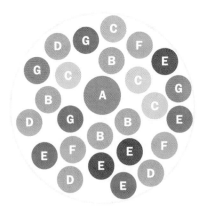

Essentials

Container: 16×11-inch heavy-gauge wire planter with a mounting base
Materials: Precut coir liner with 18 side holes; metal mounting box; wood screws; 5-foot-tall, 4×4-inch salvaged post
Light: Sun
Water: Keep soil damp

Ingredients

A. 1 angelonia (purple)
B. 4 melampodium
C. 4 fan flower (purple)
D. 4 lantana (pink; yellow)
E. 6 calibrachoa (red; purple)
F. 4 artemisia
G. 4 sweet potato (chartreuse; purple)

Notes

Start with a kit that includes a specially designed basket and mounting hardware that slides over a wooden post as shown. Other mounting hardware options are also available.

WELL HYDRATED

Prepare each plant for planting by dipping its root ball in a bucket of tepid water that contains a dose of liquid transplant fertilizer. When the soil is saturated, place the plant in the container.

Higher Calling

Planting into the sides and top of a hanging basket yields spectacular results that develop quickly. Mounted on a salvaged porch post, this planter has extra charm.

Plant one layer at a time using lightweight potting mix.

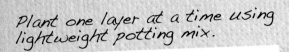

step 1

step 2

HERE'S HOW...

1 Fill your planter accordingly This wire planter and precut coir liner holds up to 18 side plants (4-inch nursery pots), 12 top-edging plants (4-inch pots), and one centerpiece plant (6-inch or gallon pots).

2 Plant in layers

Slip a plant out of its nursery pot, immerse the root ball in a bucket of water, gently squeeze it to release excess water, and tuck the root ball into a planting hole. Repeat to plant each lower side hole, completing one layer of plants.

3 Cover root balls with potting mix

Plant the second layer of side plantings; plant the centerpiece and edging, filling in between root balls after each layer. Gently sprinkle the soil with water to moisten it throughout the container. Water thoroughly after a day or two.

Avoid burying the plants' stems when planting—that could cause them to rot.

step 3

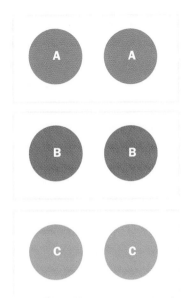

Small Is Beautiful

Turn ordinary wicker baskets into wall planters by threading heavy-gauge wire around their rims to form a supportive hanger. Apply a sealant to protect the baskets. Use a liner in each basket to hold in soil and moisture.

Essentials

Container: 11×7×7-inch basket with liner
Light: Shade to part sun
Water: Keep soil moist

Ingredients

A. 2 orange Nonstop tuberous begonia
B. 2 red Nonstop tuberous begonia
C. 2 yellow Nonstop tuberous begonia

Notes

Tuberous begonias, prized for their gorgeous vivid blooms, thrive in cool shade and moist soil. New-generation varieties, such as Nonstop and Solenia, have been developed to strut their stuff in brighter, drier, and warmer conditions.

BHG TEST GARDEN TIP

RECYCLE THOSE TUBERS

At the end of the growing season, unpot nonhardy begonia tubers and prepare to store them indoors over winter. Rinse the tubers, snip off remaining foliage, and allow the tubers to dry before packing them in damp peat moss or vermiculite. Replant in spring.

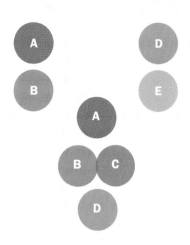

Essentials

Container: 7×6-, 10×8-, and 12×8-inch oval metal buckets
Light: Part shade
Water: Keep soil damp

Ingredients

A. 2 Bonfire dragon wing begonia
B. 2 alternanthera
C. 1 jewels of opar (*Talinum paniculatum* 'Limon')
D. 2 Tahitian bridal veil (*Tradescantia multiflora*)
E. 1 orange Nonstop tuberous begonia

Notes

Newer series of begonias, including Mandarin and Bonfire, bloom earlier and longer than true tuberous varieties, not only withstanding summer heat and humidity but preferring some sun.

CONTAINER BASICS

PERFECT FOR POTS

When you're plant shopping, keep an eye out for new varieties that offer compact growth habits, long seasons of bloom, and fun colors as well as high-performance characteristics, such as the ability to withstand extreme heat, humidity, or dry conditions.

Petal to the Metal

Display a set of pretty containers by placing them eye-high on a surface such as a fence. The arrangement works like a blank canvas, allowing you to paint with flowers and foliage.

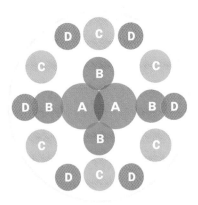

Essentials

Container: 24-inch concrete urn
Materials: 24-inch topiary frame
Light: Part shade
Water: When soil begins to feel dry

Ingredients

A. 2 English ivy
B. 4 pink impatiens
C. 6 pink-and-white ivy geraniums
D. 6 variegated plectranthus

Notes

This container gains—and gives back—impact from its placement as the centerpiece of a circular entryway pad. Alternatively, display a similar planter at the end of a path. Or flank an entryway with a pair of planters.

TEST GARDEN TIP

MEET IVY GERANIUM

Different from its zonal geranium cousins, this group of pelargoniums gets its name from its leaf shape. Choose from many types, ranging from 2 to 4 feet tall. Many have two-tone flowers.

Front & Center

An ivy topiary on a metal frame settled into the middle of the planter gives this design added height and presence, making it ideal as the head-high welcoming committee delegated to an entryway.

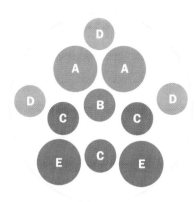

Essentials

Container: 18-inch terra-cotta pot and terra-cotta pedestal
Light: Part shade to sun
Water: When soil begins to feel dry

Ingredients

A. 2 canna
B. 1 coleus
C. 3 red ivy geranium
D. 3 pink New Guinea impatiens
E. 2 purple heart

Notes

A pedestal catches interest, then directs the eye to the potted garden it holds up. Choose a pedestal in proportion to the size and shape of the pot.

IMPROV STAGE

No need to buy a fancy pedestal to take your potted garden to a higher level. Improvise by placing pots on top of clay pipes or chimney pots, which also work well on their own as tall planters.

A Room for a View

A hedge or backdrop of other foliage sets the stage for an outstanding container garden. Planting bold contrasts in the pot using bright- and light-hued plants will help set it apart from nearby plantings

Good Neighbor Garden

A low, strong fence provides an ideal station for a planter. The container garden screens unwelcome views in a flowery way while improving the scenery.

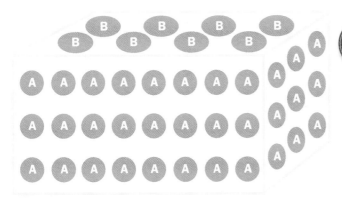

Essentials

Container: 10×20×10-inch Bloom Master planter
Light: Sun to part shade
Water: Keep soil damp

Ingredients

A. 42 ivy and zonal geranium (24 in front; 9 in each end)
B. 8 zonal and fancy-leaf geranium (in top)

Notes

The planter box combines the strength and form of a window box with the added planting holes of a hanging basket. Its design results in a mass of flowers and foliage.

BHG
PLANT
SWAP

TUMBLING GREENERY

Combine upright and mounding plants in the top and cascading plants in the sides of the planter to achieve a massed effect. Upright and mounding plant alternatives include marigold, nemesia, and torenia. Cascading plant alternatives include petunia, calibrachoa, begonia, Gem marigold, and trailing verbena.

Premoisten the potting mix before planting.

step 1

step 2

HERE'S HOW...

1 Plant the bottom layer first

Fill the planter with premoistened potting mix to the bottom edge of the bottom row of planting pockets. Water all plants before planting. Gently insert a root ball through each pocket and into the box, resting it on the potting mix. (Or plant every other hole, using half as many—but larger—seedlings.) Alternate plant varieties for a varied look.

2 Cover root balls with potting mix

Repeat planting process for the next two rows of planting pockets.

3 Fill the planter with potting mix

Tuck compact plants into the top of the planter. Wait a day or two before watering the planter thoroughly if the potting mix has begun to dry. The planter is designed so that potting mix will not wash out of the planting pockets, whether they are planted or not.

Fertilize every two weeks with water-soluble plant food.

step 3

Purple Pleaser

Well-chosen plants and planters flatter the front of a house and help make the best impression. Take a cue from the your home's trim to color coordinate a window box and planting scheme.

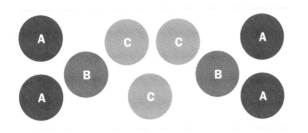

Essentials
Container: 48-inch painted cedar window box
Light: Part shade to sun
Water: Keep soil damp

Ingredients
A. 4 purple nemesia
B. 2 purple lobelia
C. 3 cascading purple petunia

Notes
Purple plant varieties coordinate easily with a lavender box. If summer heat finishes off any of these annuals, pull out the spent plants and replace them with purple fall-bloomers.

INFO CONTAINER BASICS

LONGER LIFE
Fit a plastic window box liner in the window box and plant in the liner to extend the life of the box.

Home Improvement

Follow a basic recipe when planting a window box: Mix upright, mounding, and trailing plants. If a plant has an arching form, use it to grace the ends of the display.

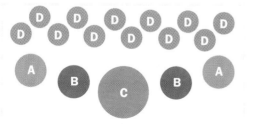

Essentials

Container: 36-inch cedar window box
Light: Part shade
Water: When soil begins to feel dry

Ingredients

A. 2 variegated lilyturf (*Liriope muscari*)
B. 2 flowering kale
C. 1 trailing verbena
D. 12 branches of snowberry (*Symphoricarpos* spp.)

Notes

Tuck fresh-cut berried branches into the container garden to add a seasonal flourish. The berries will dry gradually.

BIG CONTAINER BASICS

RAIN OR SHINE

Window boxes require attentive watering because rain will rarely do the job for you. Water from indoors, if possible, using a watering can.

Autumn Attractions

Bring the warm hues of a harvest-season sunset to linger on your windowsill. Allow for seasonal changes in a window box by fitting it with a plastic liner at planting time.

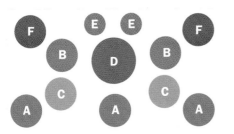

Essentials

Container: 36-inch window box with 35-inch plastic liner
Light: Part shade to sun
Water: Keep soil damp

Ingredients

A. 3 asparagus fern
B. 2 chrysanthemum ('Copper Charm')
C. 2 *Euphorbia* ('Diamond Frost')
D. 1 hydrangea ('Alpenglow')
E. 2 sedge ('Toffee Twist')
F. 2 sweet william ('Amazon Rose Magic')

Notes

The planter's vintage-look patina comes with a coat of crackling glaze followed by a top coat of milk paint.

CHANGING PLACES

When chilly weather arrives, move the ferns indoors for the winter. Transplant the other plants into the garden.

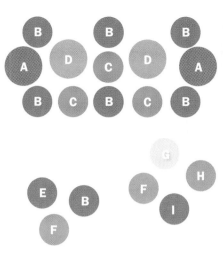

Essentials

Container: 48-inch fiberglass window box; 18-inch terra-cotta pots
Light: Part shade
Water: Keep soil damp

Ingredients

Window box

A. 2 sweet potato
B. 6 white wax begonia
C. 3 variegated English ivy
D. 2 pink trailing verbena

Terra-cotta pots

E. 1 *Eugenia* topiary
B. 1 white wax begonia
F. 2 plumbago
G. 1 *Euphorbia* ('Diamond Frost')
H. 1 pink impatiens
I. 1 trailing vinca

Notes

Repeating plant shapes and colors achieves a cohesive look with more interest than the same plantings used again and again.

FOLLOW YOUR NOSE

When planning a window box, include scented plants and then enjoy the way their sweet perfume wafts into the house. Candidates include sweet alyssum, stock, and scented geranium.

PART SHADE

Color Coordinated

Create an organized and cohesive look when combining containers at various heights within an outdoor room. Repeating pots as well as plant shapes and colors is the first step toward a clean, uncluttered setting.

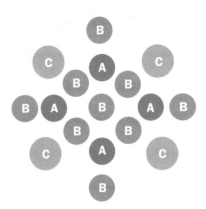

Essentials

Container: 14-inch hanging basket
Materials: 14-inch coir liner;
moisture-retentive potting mix
Light: Part shade
Water: Keep soil damp

Ingredients

A. 4 salmon single impatiens
B. 9 magenta single impatiens
C. 4 lilac single impatiens

Notes

Annuals in multipacks are easiest to plug into side- and bottom-planted baskets. Single impatiens grows to about 10 inches, with multiple branching stems, forming a billowing globe of flowers and foliage. Understanding a plant's growth habit enables you to use it to advantage.

BHG CONTAINER BASICS

LINER OPTIONS

The type of liner you choose for a hanging basket can help minimize its inevitable moisture loss and help plants survive and thrive. Coir (coconut-husk fiber), sphagnum peat moss, and compressed wood fiber are among popular options. Try a newer option made from moisture-retentive plant fibers.

Summer Splendor

Gorgeous hanging baskets are within your reach, especially when you begin by choosing dependable plants. Selecting different colors of impatiens gives you a simple-but-effective option for a shaded location.

Pot of Gold

A jackpot of color emanates from a hanging basket that includes only three selections of cascading plants in different tints of one color. A top-planted basket uses fewer plants and produces a slimmer silhouette.

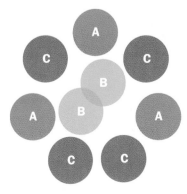

Essentials

Container: 12-inch hanging basket
Materials: 12-inch moisture-holding liner; moisture-retentive potting mix; birdhouse, if desired
Light: Part shade to sun
Water: Keep soil damp

Ingredients

A. 3 creeping zinnia ('Aztec Gold')
B. 2 petunia (Supertunia 'Citrus')
C. 4 calibrachoa (Superbells Yellow)

Notes

Drip irrigation helps you tend to the high water needs of hanging baskets. Otherwise, use a watering wand for easier reach.

BIG
CONTAINER
BASICS

HANG IT UP

If you can't lift potted plantings without strain, they're likely too heavy to suspend from a hook. Hang a basket using a swivel snap hook that allows you to turn the container periodically to ensure even light exposure.

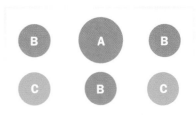

Essentials

Container: 28×10×10-inch fiberglass planter
Materials: 2×6-foot copper trellis
Light: Part shade
Water: Keep soil damp

Ingredients

A. 1 clock vine *(Thunbergia grandiflora)*
B. 3 variegated English ivy
C. 2 yellow viola

Notes

A trellis gives vines a boost up, supporting them as they grow. The vigorous vines clambers up and over the fence, decorating both sides of it.

PLANT SWAP

ALTERNATIVE PLANTINGS

Employ pairs of fast-growing vines for a more colorful and dramatic focal point, such as black-eyed susan vine with nasturtium, or jasmine with creeping gloxinia *(Lophospermum erubescens, aka Asarina scandens).*

Over the Fence

A container enables you to plant on top of a hard surface, then count on vines to grow up and adorn an otherwise drab adjacent fence. Add color at the base of the climbing plant using annuals and variegated ivy.

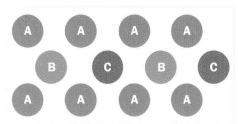

Essentials

Container: 36×12×12-inch cedar planter boxes
Materials: 7-foot rebar rods; 36-inch-wide wire rabbit fencing; wire
Light: Part shade to shade
Water: Keep soil damp

Ingredients

A. 8 English ivy
B. 2 yellow gazania
C. 2 red multiflora petunia

Notes

Stand the rods upright in the corners of the planter. Stretch the rabbit fencing taut between the uprights, securing it to them with twists of wire. Add staked candleholders to the planter for a finishing touch.

BHG CONTAINER BASICS

IVY VARIETIES

If you can't find a pleasing variety of ivy at a garden center or nursery, look for it at a florist's or where houseplants are sold.

Ivy League

Planters' portability means you can grow plants almost anywhere. In this setting, movable containers help create privacy on an exposed patio. Make two or more planters and set them close together to form a wall.

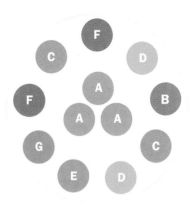

Yellow and Mellow

Monochromatic schemes make it easy to choose plants. This collection of plants with yellow flowers or yellow-variegated foliage creates a tub of sunshine on wheels.

Essentials
Container: 18-inch redwood or cedar planter
Materials: Three 4-foot-tall garden stakes; finial, if desired; dolly
Light: Part shade
Water: Keep soil damp

Ingredients
A. 3 black-eyed susan vine
B. 1 variegated flowering maple
C. 2 heliopsis ('Loraine Sunshine')
D. 2 trailing vinca ('Illumination')
E. 1 lantana ('Samantha')
F. 2 variegated potato vine
(Solanum jasminoides)
G. 1 coleus

Notes
Setting the planter on a sturdy dolly makes it easy to move into more or less sunlight. Secure the stake tops using a cap or wire. Plant a vine at the base of each stake.

TERRIFIC TRELLISES
When you add a climbing or vining plant to a container garden, grow the plant vertically to gain visual impact.

Start with your favorite
vine and let it inspire the
planting scheme.

step 1

step 2

HERE'S HOW...

1 Lean on a painted trellis

A fragrant Madagascar jasmine gets plenty
of support from a painted trellis leaning
against the wall behind the potted plant.

2 Salvage a support from nature

A variegated morning glory vine puts on a
dramatic show all by itself. Given a windfall
branch for support, the vine reaches high
for the sky.

3 Use ties to keep up vines

Bamboo stakes capped with small terra-cotta
pots make neat trellises for tomato plants in
18-inch pots. Tie the vines to the stakes to
secure them.

Get bolder color with
flowering plants or
brightly painted pots.

step 3

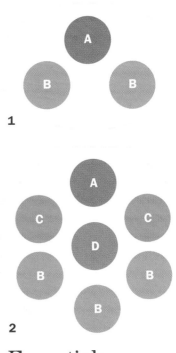

1

2

Essentials

Container: 14-inch footed cast-iron planter; 20-inch cast-iron planter on pedestal
Light: Shade
Water: Keep soil damp

Ingredients

Pot 1
A. 1 maidenhair fern
B. 2 pansy

Pot 2
A. 1 maidenhair fern
B. 3 pansy
C. 2 English ivy
D. 1 hosta

Notes

Select containers that echo one another's color or shape for one of the easiest and most pleasing designs possible. Repeat some of the plantings to reinforce the effect.

BHG
PLANT
SWAP

ALTERNATIVE PLANTINGS

For colorful plantings in shade, try: double impatiens (bright, plump flowers), caladium (showy foliage), and fuchsia (dangling flowers).

Making an Entrance

Plants enhance any entryway, bringing lively, continuous color to it. Raising the plantings closer to eye level makes them all the more welcoming (and able to receive light in this setting).

Facing North

Visible from indoors, a bright and colorful container brings cheer to the shady side of a house. The copper box and steel frame are made to last and sized to fit a standard window frame.

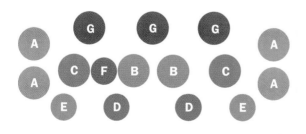

Essentials

Container: 36-inch steel window box frame with copper liner
Light: Shade
Water: Keep soil damp

Ingredients

A. 4 impatiens
B. 2 jacob's ladder ('Brise d'Anjou')
C. 2 hosta
D. 2 variegated ground ivy
E. 2 purple plectranthus
F. 1 sweet potato
G. 3 upright fuchsia

Notes

Choose a window box that's at least 8 inches deep to give plant roots room to grow and to save you from watering more than once a day during hot weather.

CONTAINER BASICS

PROPER MOUNTING

Prevent future problems and damage to your house by properly mounting a window box. Using sturdy brackets or lag bolts (and lead anchors in a brick house), secure the box to the wall rather than the window trim.

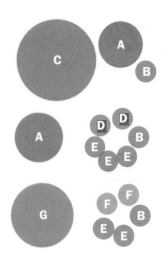

Essentials

Container: Six 12- to 16-inch glazed ceramic pots
Light: Sun to part shade
Water: When soil begins to feel dry

Ingredients

A. 2 croton
B. 3 sweet potato
C. 1 hosta ('Sum and Substance')
D. 2 lantana
E. 5 pink vinca
F. 2 dusty miller
G. 1 sedum ('Autumn Joy')

Notes

This garden in containers succeeds in part because the plant selection focuses on the entire composition rather than on individual pots. Repetition of chartreuse and pink tie the container plantings together in a pleasing combination of bold foliage and bright blooms.

LITTLE ECHOES

After you've filled the nooks and crannies of your flowerbeds with favorite annuals, tuck leftover plants into pots that will coordinate with the garden.

Step Right Up

Achieve fast, high-impact color in a compact space such as steps at an entry or a small deck by grouping pots at the perimeter. Keep plantings simple by placing one or two varieties in each pot, then move pots around to achieve the desired overall effect. Leave plenty of room for foot traffic.

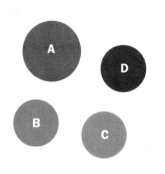

Essentials

Container: 24×50-inch glazed pot
Light: Shade
Water: When soil begins to feel dry

Ingredients

A. 1 dwarf Japanese maple
B. 1 toad lily *(Tricyrtis hirta)*
C. 1 moneywort ('Goldilocks')
D. 1 mondo grass *(Ophiopogon)*

Notes

The slow-growing tree and its perennial companions were selected for their foliage textures and colors through the seasons.

TREES, PLEASE

When you plan to add instant height to a potted garden with a dwarf tree or shrub, start with a young plant and allow plenty of room for its roots to grow inside the container. Eventually, the tree or shrub will outgrow the pot and need to be transplanted into the landscape.

Little Landscape

Combine a small character-rich tree such as a dwarf Japanese maple with an understory of plants in a large pot to take advantage of vertical space. You'll want varieties that are hardy in your region.

CHAPTER FIVE

More Impact, Less Work

Shaped compact boxwoods in 12-inch pots bring structure and a sense of order to a garden. Ensure the prosperity of an attention-getter such as this in sun or shade with regular watering.

Set your sights on colorful container gardens that will energize your landscape throughout the year. Use the recipes in this chapter to expand your planting horizons while simplifying the ways you do it. You'll soon discover the secrets to creating unforgettable potted gardens in minutes and continuing your success for years to come.

Easy Does It

When you take a simplified approach to creating container gardens, chances are you'll enjoy the process more without feeling overwhelmed or underfunded. The easiest schemes typically include a restrained plant selection. Many of the recipes shown on the pages ahead are quick to make yet sure to attain maximum impact, using easy-care plants with long-lasting flowers or showy foliage.

Some of the most efficient container gardens fulfill more than one purpose: The plants are decorative and edible, or they combine a water feature with plantings, for instance. Your container garden might function as garden art, outdoor lighting, or long-term landscaping.

Sustainable gardens include plants, such as perennials or shrubs, which can live for several years in containers, needing minimal maintenance and resources. They may feature native plants, provide a food source or habitat for wildlife, or live in harmony with nature throughout the seasons. Your sustainable garden's health relies on organic gardening techniques with positive environmental consequences.

Special effects

Creating instant, entertaining, or surprising effects with containers depends on your planting choices. Whether large or small, dramatic or subtle, some plants are too wonderful to be appreciated anywhere but as stars in potted habitats.

Containers often provide ideal homes for special plants that benefit from nurturing before settling into larger garden life. The container itself makes an artful statement, while the planting provides a finishing touch.

The most special containers often have qualities and effects beyond our conception. The wonders of water—especially moving water—and plants combined in a pot never cease to intrigue. Arranged like cut flowers for special occasions, some potted displays decorate a tabletop or accent an entry in a way that greets guests and makes them feel welcome. Some containers entertain with their novelty; others boost spirits with their enduring appeal.

right Decorate a tabletop in a flash with temporary plantings of young ornamental grasses, such as annual 'Pink Crystals' ruby grass (Melinus nerviglumis).

below Dynamic combinations of purple and yellow annuals, including zinnia, verbena, heliotrope, and Persian shield, add color to a patio. Garden torches stand in the pots and light the place at night.

opposite Windows look out on a patio garden. The potted collection includes vacationing houseplants as well as purple fountain grass and a colonnade apple tree.

Potted Water Gardens

A water garden offers more benefits than meet the eye. First, it introduces to you and visitors a world of fascinating water-loving plants not ordinarily found in container gardens. Add the gentle, soothing sound of trickling water to a potted garden and you'll multiply the pleasures it brings in other ways: The sound creates a relaxing ambience, masks obtrusive noise such as nearby traffic, and entices birds to take a dip or a drink.

Whether using a potted water garden is a year-round asset in a mild climate or for temporary beauty in a colder region, anyone can appreciate the minimal expense and maintenance involved. Set up your potted water garden and start reaping the rewards in an afternoon.

Do it yourself

Any container will work as long as it is watertight and at least 6 inches deep. A 12-inch bowl holds potential for delight, especially when situated on a tabletop. A larger, deeper container can host a wider variety of plants along with a fountain while serving as a striking feature in the landscape.

Place your potted water garden where you'll enjoy it the most. Consider raising it above ground level or using a tall container to make it easily seen and heard. Keep the container within reach of a hose so you can replenish its water regularly.

Situate water-loving plants at their preferred depth with roots submerged or crowns (growing points) floating on the water's surface. Plant tags should help you determine the best growing conditions for your plants. Start with only two or three plants if the container's diameter is 18 inches or less. Feature a single type of plant or a variety in a larger container to achieve different effects.

You'll find details to help you make a potted water garden that includes a small fountain on pages 176–177.

Large galvanized containers of cattails catch water from a wall fountain. The patterned planting would be effective even without the fountain element.

top A large, sturdy glazed pot becomes a stunning water feature and home to a lotus. **above** If you live in a cold-winter climate, treat water lettuce, dwarf umbrella plant, elephant's ear 'Black Magic', and other plants as annuals. Empty, clean, and store the pot before freezing weather arrives.

Sustainable Schemes

If your goal includes saving time, effort, or money, then it pays to understand how to make potted gardens that span the seasons. Get to know the plants among the perennials, shrubs, and trees that can live for several years in containers without requiring replacement. Highlight a container garden with at least one long-lived plant, whether it is evergreen or deciduous, and you'll save yourself the work of completely redoing a container in the spring.

Where the climate is conducive, marathon plants offer year-round impact. Where the climate proves challenging to the plants' survival in a pot, you don't have to treat these long-lived plants as annuals and toss them on the compost pile once freezing weather arrives. Wherever you live, it's possible to practice plant conservation, using careful planning and storage techniques to overwinter plants.

Think outside the box

Extend the longevity of your container gardens by turning to a greater array of planting options beyond annuals. Take advantage of plants you might not ordinarily think of using in containers, such as self-sufficient ornamental grasses, color-rich conifers, and long-flowering shrubs. Then play upon their architectural aspects. A woody vine or tree-form standard adds instant verticality to a design. Houseplants and succulents add appreciable contrasts in leaf size, texture, and color.

Containers provide an excellent opportunity to experiment with plants and learn more about how they behave and what they need. Consider the plants' ultimate sizes when planting and make sure the chosen container won't be overwhelmed by a plant as it matures. Beware of vigorous and spreading plants that will rapidly outgrow containers, exhaust the soil, and demand repotting or replacing. In the end, your favorite plants will likely include some that ask little but give much and earn a place in your permanent garden.

right Tiger Eyes is a well-behaved staghorn sumac *(Rhus typhina)* with brilliant foliage and a compact form that's ideal for a container.
below Incorporating a young tree (ginkgo), a perennial (lilyturf), and an annual (fan flower) in a container expands your plant repertoire and allows you to see how plants with intriguing foliage bring lasting interest to groupings.
opposite A vintage copper washtub hosts a shade garden, including Japanese maple, hosta, coleus, and tassel fern.

Keeping Up Appearances

Practice a few basic gardening techniques to keep long-term potted gardens looking their best and extend your enjoyment of them. Read about general container care in the next chapter and also keep in mind these tips pertaining to your sustainable pots:

Choose a spacious, sturdy, and frost-free container to accommodate plants destined for long-term relationships.

Start with high-quality, compost-enriched potting mix. Top off the potting mix in a container periodically as watering erodes it. Replenish long-term plantings by replacing at least one-third of the loose potting mix with a fresh, compost-enriched blend.

Feed plants by adding a time-release fertilizer to the potting mix at planting time. Supplement with a dose of liquid fertilizer as needed during growth periods.

After planting, cover the soil with an inch of mulch and tuck in drip irrigation to ensure soil moisture.

Remove spent flowers and leaves; lightly prune plants as needed to maintain their overall appearance.

In cold climates, give planters shelter and extra protection to help them survive winter. Water plants occasionally throughout winter. Read more about winter protection in Chapter 6.

Potted water gardens require specific attention to water quality and winterization.

above Easy-care Scotch moss carpets the soil of a potted lemon tree and demonstrates the creative use of a groundcover.
opposite Small-leaved boxwood and rosemary can be clipped into simple, geometric shapes using hand pruners or small hedge shears.

BHG CONTAINER BASICS

IN THE ZONE When selecting plants for your potted gardens, choose ones that will be container-hardy in your zone, meaning ones that are two zones hardier than the zone where you live (see zone maps on page 218). If you live in Zone 5, for example, choose plants that are designated as hardy to Zone 3 to help ensure their survival in a container garden. If you're willing to experiment with plants, they might surprise you by flourishing in a protected location with a microclimate that equates to one zone warmer—on a sunny enclosed patio or next to the south side of the house, for instance.

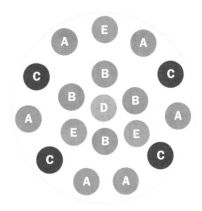

Essentials

Container: 20-inch stone-look urn
Light: Sun
Water: When soil begins to feel dry

Ingredients
(for each container)

A. 6 pale pink petunia (trailing type)
B. 4 licorice plant ('Splash')
C. 4 black-purple sweet potato
D. 1 pale pink geranium
E. 3 licorice plant ('Icicles')

Notes

Many newer petunia varieties don't require deadheading, but they will benefit from pinching occasionally and shearing by one-third in midseason. Monthly feeding helps keep petunias blooming all summer. Overwatering can cause plants to become leggy (with lots of stems and few flowers).

TEST GARDEN TIP

BLOOMING ON AND ON

Besides petunia, include any of these long-blooming annuals in your container gardens for nonstop flowers from spring into fall: dianthus, marigold, salvia, snapdragon, verbena, wax begonia, and zinnia.

Marathon Bloomers

A pair of large containers standing at eye level and flanking a front walk will wow passersby as well as visitors with a profusion of annuals that bloom continously throughout the growing season. Those who come close will be rewarded with the sweet scent of petunias.

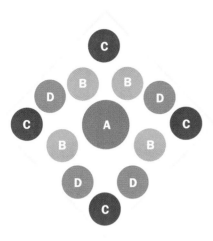

Essentials

Container: 2 salvaged metal corner pieces screwed and wired together to form a box
Light: Sun
Water: When soil feels dry

Ingredients

A. 1 purple beautyberry (*Callicarpa dichotoma* 'Issai')
B. 4 pink chrysanthemum
C. 4 ornamental cabbage
D. 4 creeping wire vine (*Muehlenbeckia axillaris*)

Notes

Cornices and decorative moldings from the tops of dismantled old buildings are too precious for the junk pile. Visit salvage businesses and flea markets to find bits of antique architecture worth preserving, then convert them into a planter using a little resourcefulness, a few screws, and some wire.

ADAPTABLE SHRUB

Outstanding among shrubs, purple beautyberry extends the length of the display into winter with berried branches that attract birds. When grown in containers, most shrubs reach less than their normal size.

SUN

Seasoned Showcase

Turning salvaged cornices into an elegant planter creates a high-impact entryway garden. Filled with soil, the architectural accent sits on top of a brick pedestal and shows off long-season plantings.

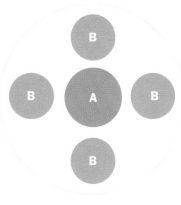

Essentials
Container: 12×22-inch earthenware jar
Light: Sun
Water: When soil feels dry

Ingredients
A. 1 fountain grass ('Hameln')
B. 4 Mexican feather grass
(*Nassella tenuissima* 'Ponytails')

Notes
Ornamental grasses need no more than a dose of a slow-release fertilizer worked into the potting mix at planting time to see them through the growing season.

BIG TEST GARDEN TIP

HALE AND HARDY
Like other long-term plants, ornamental grasses lose zones of hardiness when they spend the winter in a container. Fountain grass and feather grass in this recipe, which are ordinarily hardy to Zone 4, should be able to survive the winter in a pot in Zone 6. Otherwise, transfer the plants to your garden in early fall.

Leaves of Grass

Ornamental grasses blend subtle colors with airy textures in all-season displays. They outperform flowers by creating poetry in motion with their dancing forms and rustling sounds. For best results, combine an upright grass with an arching variety. Choose grasses with similar requirements for light and water.

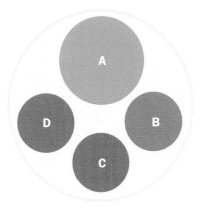

Essentials

Container: 20-inch synthetic urn
Light: Sun
Water: Keep soil damp

Ingredients

A. 1 lemongrass
B. 1 bacopa ('Snowstorm Pink')
C. 1 heuchera ('Dolce Mocha Mint')
D. 1 gooseneck loosestrife
(*Lysimachia clethroides*
'Snow Candle')

Notes

Harvest perennial lemongrass in
late summer or early fall and use
it in cooking or for making tea.
Start next year's crop by saving a
stalk or two with roots attached;
cut off the greenest portion and
replant the root end. Keep the
plant indoors through the winter.

PLANT SWAP

ALTERNATIVE PLANTINGS

Replace the lemongrass with
another perennial grass that will
take beautifully to container life,
such as *Calamagrostis (feather
reed grass), Festuca (fescue),
Miscanthus (porcupinegrass),* or
Panicum (switch grass).

SUN

Long-term Lease

Lemongrass, a tropical herb hardy to Zone 9,
flourishes throughout the growing season in a
container and then gives you a bonus: a harvest
of edible stalks, popular in many types of Asian
and Caribbean cooking.

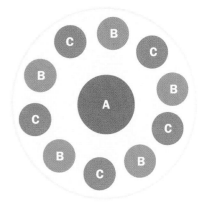

Essentials
Container: 24-inch fiberglass urn
Light: Sun
Water: When soil begins to feel dry

Ingredients
(for each container)
A. 1 dwarf globe arborvitae
B. 5 stonecrop *(Sedum spathulifolium* 'Cape Blanco')
C. 5 chartreuse coleus

Notes
Shrubs and perennials bring self-sufficient qualities to container gardens. Dwarf arborvitae keeps its globe shape with little or no trimming. Leave the easy-care evergreen and sedum in the container year after year and merely replace the coleus annually. Pinch back the coleus' tips regularly to limit their height and keep them dense.

DID YOU KNOW?

EASY EVERGREENS
Blending compost into the potting mix at planting time helps ensure an evergreen's health and longevity. No other fertilizer is necessary.

Ever Green

A slow-growing dwarf conifer forms a ruffled green centerpiece in this year-round container scheme. The petite shrub will harmonize with most settings as well as with its companion plantings and remain contentedly in the pot for several years.

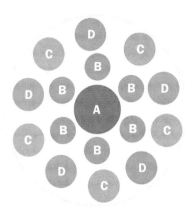

Essentials

Container: 18-inch terra-cotta standard pot
Light: Sun
Water: When soil begins to feel dry

Ingredients

A. 1 boxwood topiary
B. 6 pink vinca
C. 5 lavender lobelia
D. 5 dichondra ('Silver Falls')

Notes

Many gardeners shape boxwood with an electric hedge trimmer, but it's best to pinch or clip the branch tips. Trimming each stem at the junction of another stem encourages better form as new growth develops naturally from several places. Trim boxwood in early spring and late summer.

BHG TEST GARDEN TIP

TOPS IN TOPIARY

Boxwood's ability to handle shaping makes it a classic choice for topiary forms. Start with a preformed shrub in a shape you desire, such as a lollipop or cone. Choose a slow-growing, cold-hardy variety such as 'Little Gem' if appropriate in the climate where you live.

SUN

On the Ball

Choose boxwood to anchor a potted garden with its sturdy evergreen appeal. As a shrub, boxwood offers versatility of form and a foil for color contrasts. As living sculpture, it has been called the world's oldest garden ornament.

Sun Dance

Carefree succulents are naturals for containers. With their laid-back personalities, the plants thrive in toasty, well-drained environs. Succulents' fleshy, water-storing leaves earn them their catchall name as well as high praise for creating fascinating textures.

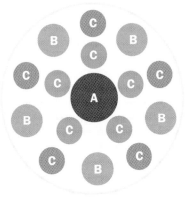

Essentials

Container: 18-inch terra-cotta bowl
Light: Sun
Water: Allow soil to dry between waterings. Water sparingly through winter months

Ingredients

A. 1 giant echeveria
B. 5 echeveria ('Silver Spoons', 'Perle von Nurnberg',
and *E. shaviana*)
C. 10 golden sedum

Notes

Plant succulents in a potting mix blended with sand and gravel. Regular potting mix holds too much moisture. In hot, sunny locales, give plants afternoon shade. Move nonhardy succulents indoors over winter in cold climates and keep them near a sunny window.

CAN-DO DESIGN

MYRIAD CHOICES

Part of the fun in designing container gardens of succulents comes in choosing from the vast array of plant varieties and then planting them in a geometric pattern. Multiply echeverias and similar species by transferring their new little rosettes into small pots of sandy potting mix.

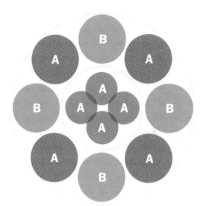

Essentials

Container: Two-tier concrete fountain
Light: Sun
Water: Allow soil to dry between waterings

Ingredients

Top bowl:

A. 4 stringy stonecrop (*Sedum sarmentosum*)

Bottom bowl:

A. 4 stringy stonecrop (*Sedum sarmentosum*)
B. 4 two-row stonecrop (*Sedum spurium* 'John Creech')

Notes

Before planting, cover the bottom of each bowl with pea gravel to enhance drainage. Both sedum varieties creep and trail by nature, spreading via their shallow roots and filling the planters within a season. They'll gradually "trickle" over the planters' edges.

ALTERNATIVE PLANTINGS

Mature succulents will flower, but the plants are typically most valued for their foliage. If you want flowers, plant moss rose (*Portulaca*), a drought-tolerant annual, in your fountain.

Creative Splash

Take advantage of hardy succulents' penchant for well-draining, sun-baked conditions and then transform a worn fountain (without a water supply) into a planter for them. From spring through fall, the fountain will once again overflow with life.

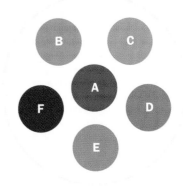

Essentials

Container: 16-inch terra-cotta bowl
Light: Sun
Water: When soil feels dry

Ingredients

A. 1 chives
B. 1 rosemary
C. 1 sage
D. 1 marjoram
E. 1 thyme
F. 1 globe basil

Notes

Keep small scissors nearby
for snipping bits of herbs to
sprinkle on food or use in grilling.
Transplant the herbs to your
garden when their growth slows
and they need more room for
developing roots.

PLANT SWAP

ALTERNATIVE PLANTINGS

Plant a sweet herb bowl—
including peppermint, orange
mint, stevia, and scented
geranium—and keep it handy for
snipping, especially when dessert
is served.

Savory Centerpiece

Most herbs grow happily in containers, where
they will reward you with their delightful
scents and flavors. A snip-and-eat centerpiece
keeps savory herbs where they will stimulate
conversation as well as taste buds in the
midst of meals outdoors.

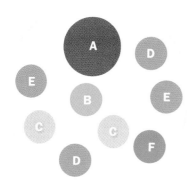

Essentials

Container: 19-inch metal urn
Light: Sun
Water: When the soil feels dry

Ingredients

A. 1 rose ('Little Mischief')
B. 1 petunia ('Carpet Buttercream')
C. 2 white bacopa
D. 2 verbena ('Peaches and Cream')
E. 2 apricot diascia
F. 1 variegated trailing vinca

Notes

A container provides ideal growing conditions for a rose: compost-rich soil, ample water, consistent fertilizer, plenty of room for healthy root growth, good drainage, and a location with adequate light and air circulation.

COLD CARE

If the ground freezes during winter in your region, transplant your rose into the garden in late summer and keep it well watered throughout fall. In late summer and fall, avoid feeding and cutting roses, which would encourage new tender growth easily damaged during winter.

Harmonic Convergence

Yes, you can grow roses successfully in containers! Compact 2- to 3-foot-tall landscape roses are particularly well suited to pots. Choose a hardy rose that will bloom all summer, and complement it with plant partners that will flower at its feet.

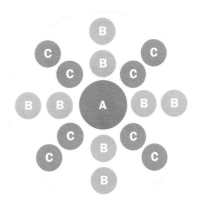

Essentials

Container: 18-inch terra-cotta pot
Light: Sun
Water: When soil begins to feel dry

Ingredients

A. 1 pink miniature rose standard
B. 8 pink vinca
C. 8 pink wax begonia

Notes

Roses grow best in full sun with 1 inch of rain per week (or 1 gallon of water). Use a water-soluble fertilizer once a week or granular food monthly. Alfalfa pellets worked into the soil are an organic source of nitrogen and can be used as a slow-release supplement in spring. Use pellets that are not feed-grade so your rose food doesn't feed the rabbits.

BIG PLANT SWAP

ALTERNATIVE PLANTINGS

A range of flowering shrubs, dwarf evergreens, tropicals, and others adapt beautifully as standards and have become widely available at nurseries and garden centers. They include lilac, hydrangea, butterfly bush (*Buddleia*), dwarf blue spruce (*Picea pungens* 'Globosa'), lantana, and citrus.

Raising Standards

Elevate your garden style with shrubs trained to stand out. Roses reign supreme as a favorite among those grown and pruned into standards, or tree forms. Make it easy by starting with a ready-made rose standard.

Remove any new shoots from the trunk to help keep the standard's shape.

step 1

step 2

HERE'S HOW...

1 Choose a sturdy, frostproof pot
Insulated and synthetic pots dry out less quickly than terra-cotta. Prevent a standard from toppling in wind by lining the pot's bottom with rocks when planting.

2 Secure the trunk to a strong stake
Use soft ties placed about a foot apart—one near the top and one near the base of the trunk. Snip spent flowers throughout the growing season to encourage reblooming.

3 Prepare for winter
In early fall, transplant the rose to the garden in a frosty climate. Wrap the trunk with a pre-slit foam pipe insulation. Cut the top of the insulation into fingers and wrap those over the grafted area. Wrap the works with duct tape to secure it.

Insulate the trunk to protect a standard from freezing weather.

step 3

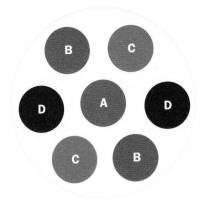

Essentials

Container: 20-inch polystyrene pot
Light: Sun
Water: When soil begins to feel dry

Ingredients

A. 1 firethorn (*Pyracantha coccinea* 'Kasan')
B. 2 lantana ('Citrus Blend')
C. 2 geranium ('Vancouver Centennial')
D. 2 coleus ('Wizard')

Notes

Grow a miniature landscape by placing a young shrub or tree in a container with a few choice accompaniments. This is a great way to try new plants and plant combinations that you might like to have in your larger landscape.

CONTAINER BASICS

TOTE THAT POT

When potting a shrub or tree, use a container that's large enough to accommodate root development but lightweight enough for the container garden to be portable.

Hot Stuff

Bring instant impact to a container garden with a hardy shrub or tree. Then put the star plant to work wherever its height will serve a purpose: Accenting an entrance, camouflaging part of a wall, or adding an interesting feature to a flowerbed.

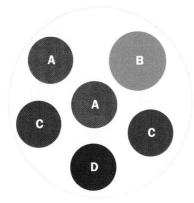

Essentials
Container: 18-inch terra-cotta pot with pot feet
Light: Sun
Water: When the soil feels dry

Ingredients
A. 2 blue salvia ('Evolution')
B. 1 canna ('Bengal Tiger')
C. 2 calibrachoa ('Mini Famous Double Blue')
D. 1 butterfly bush (*Buddleia* 'Blue Chip')

Notes
Dwarf or slow-growing varieties of shrubs and trees make ideal candidates for container gardens. In warm climates, they'll typically thrive for several years before outgrowing the pot. Refresh the soil annually. When the soil dries out at increasingly shorter intervals, transplant the shrub or tree into the garden.

NURSERY TIME
Economize by purchasing immature shrubs and small trees in 1-gallon or smaller pots. Nurture them in container gardens for a year or two before giving them a permanent home in the landscape.

SUN

Butterfly Ball

A dwarf variety of butterfly bush proves perfect for a sustainable container garden. Leave it in the container from year to year, but experiment with combinations and change out the other plants. If you like, include other plants that attract butterflies.

C D A A A
          E E F

A B
A B
A B

Essentials

Container: Cedar planters lined with sheets of foam insulation and foam packing peanuts layered in the bottom
Light: Sun
Water: Using drip irrigation, when soil feels dry

Ingredients

A. 6 boxwood
B. 3 crimson barberry
C. 1 river birch
D. 1 variegated euonymous
E. 2 lavender
F. 1 yellow daylily

Notes

The weight of containers, plants, and wet soil is a significant consideration when planning a rooftop garden. Consult building management and a landscape architect to determine how much weight the structure can hold. Your rooftop garden will also need a water source and a way to channel drainage.

CONTAINER BASICS

WEATHER REPORT

High winds, strong light, and excessive heat and cold constitute harsh conditions for any rooftop garden. Understand sun and shade patterns and wind exposure before selecting plants.

Rooftop Rules

Savvy plant choices will help make the garden ready to withstand harsh conditions as well as space efficient. Transform the ordinarily barren landscape of a rooftop or balcony into an urban oasis with lush, lovely plantings.

Essentials

Container: Cypress planter with liner
Light: Sun
Water: Using drip irrigation, when soil feels dry

Ingredients

A. 4 bamboo (clumping type)

Notes

Bamboo addresses key issues on a rooftop garden: It forms a privacy screen that also shelters a portion of the rooftop from wind. Upright and dense, bamboo stands up to strong winds better than some trees.

CONTAINER BASICS

PERSISTENT PLANTERS

The best wooden rooftop planters are made to last decades. The liners should be adequately supported and properly drained. Use a lightweight potting mix that includes peat moss and vermiculite or perlite to help ensure adequate soil drainage.

SUN

High Achievers

The most successful rooftop container garden strikes a balance between plants and square footage, leaving room for people to move around and enjoy the views. Bamboo grows quickly to add privacy and interest.

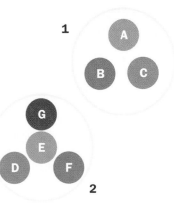

1

A

B   C

G

E

D   F

2

Essentials

Container: Two 15-inch terra-cotta pots
Light: Part shade
Water: When the soil feels dry

Ingredients

Pot 1
A. 1 eastern hemlock
B. 1 heuchera ('Dolce Crème Brûlée')
C. 1 moneywort ('Aurea')

Pot 2
D. 1 sedum ('Angelina')
E. 1 blue fescue ('Elijah Blue')
F. 1 oregano ('Kent Beauty')
G. 1 juniper ('Holger')

Notes

Cold-hardy perennials rally round young conifers, enlivening the dragonscale planters continuously for a year or two in mild regions. Unless frostproof, in frigid climates your pots should be emptied and stored and the plants given permanent places in the garden.

TEST GARDEN TIP

LABELS ARE TELLING

If the plant label doesn't specify a hardiness-zone range, you cannot be sure of the plant's viability in your region. Think twice about the purchase, unless you know the plant or intend to grow it as an annual.

Home Sweet Home

These low-maintenance gardens feature easy-care plants with moderate growth rates, few pest or disease problems, and little upkeep besides watering. The all-foliage compositions boast bright hues and contrasting textures. A seasonal prop adds an element of fun.

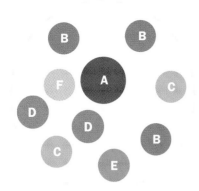

Essentials

Container: 22-inch fiberglass planter
Light: Part shade
Water: When soil begins to feel dry

Ingredients

A. 1 weeping blue atlas cedar ('Glauca Pendula')
B. 3 kale
C. 2 licorice plant
D. 2 blue flax
E. 1 blue fescue ('Elijah Blue')
F. 1 dusty miller

Notes

When a tree has been trained to exhibit an unusual form, it will likely come from the nursery attached to a sturdy stake. Leave the tree secured to this stake when transplanting the works into a new container. If the stake is flimsy, carefully replace it and secure the tree to a new support using soft ties.

YEAR IN, YEAR OUT

When you're looking for plants that will live contentedly in a container year round, include a slow-growing tree or shrub. Possibilities include dwarf (meaning slow-growing or smaller than full-size species when mature) cultivars of evergreens, such as balsam fir, false cypress, juniper, mugo pine, and spruce.

PART SHADE

Evergreen Grace

Guided by a stout stake, a topiary's artful form takes advantage of the tree's naturally pendent branchlets. The evergreen's companions highlight and echo it with silvery and blue-gray foliage. The container makes its own strong statement.

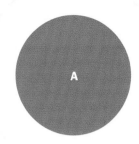

Essentials
Container: 20-inch fiberglass pot
Light: Part shade
Water: When soil feels dry

Ingredients
A. 1 upright dwarf juniper ('Hetz')

Notes
Start with a large (5- to 6-foot-tall) tree that's destined to reach a mature height of 15 feet unless you continually prune its central leader (main stem or trunk). Younger—smaller—trees cost less but will take more years to reach maturity.

PLANT SWAP

ALTERNATIVE PLANTINGS
Dwarf Alberta spruce and boxwood also make good candidates for spiral-shape topiaries.

Twisted & Stout

An evergreen topiary adds personality to a garden. You can create a spiral-form juniper for a fraction of what the ready-made ones cost at garden centers. Or you can start with a precut spiral and when it's time for upkeep, let the cuts made at the nursery be your guide.

Gain confidence by starting with a 36-inch tree and shaping a smaller topiary.

step 1

step 2

HERE'S HOW...

1 Start at the bottom

Use masking tape to mark the areas that will be left; plan to cut areas in between the tape. Use sharp pruners to begin clipping the tree, working from the middle down and then up. Proceed slowly. Step back often and walk around the tree to view it from all sides.

2 Avoid cutting aggressively

Cutting close to bare wood removes greenery permanently; cutting near the branch tips encourages bushiness over time. Rough out the spiral, then remove the tape and refine the remaining greenery, shaping it into a rounded form using shears. The tree will look crude at first.

3 Prepare for winter

In Zones 7 and warmer, the tree can grow in a pot year round. In colder regions, transplant the tree to the garden in early fall. Or move the potted tree to a protected place over winter.

Maintain the spiral form with spring and late-summer trims.

step 3

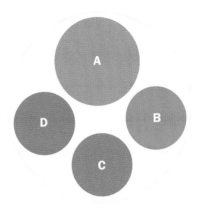

Essentials

Container: 20-inch cast-iron urn
Light: Part shade
Water: When the soil feels dry; pour water into the vaselike center of bromeliads

Ingredients

A. 1 New Zealand flax (Rainbow hybrid)
B. 1 lotus vine
C. 1 bromeliad
D. 1 croton

Notes

This garden is a natural in Zones 9–11, where these plants live outdoors year round, but it would be spectacular indoors too.

CAN-DO DESIGN

RULE OF THIRDS

Let an accent or focal plant reach high and claim one-third of the design. Let one plant balance the effect as a low element, while the supporting players fill out the design's other one-third.

Leaps & Bounds

Compatibility with your home's architecture is key when placing a potted garden near a front door and wall. As planted, this vintage urn complements a Mediterranean-style home. It would suit many modern suburban landscapes, especially those with paved outdoor spaces and hot, dry conditions.

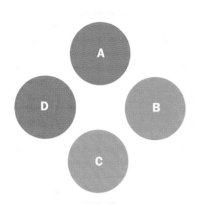

Essentials

Container: 24-inch glazed ceramic pot
Light: Part shade to sun
Water: When soil feels dry

Ingredients

A. 1 giant Burmese honeysuckle
B. 1 bacopa
C. 1 Santa Barbara daisy
D. 1 lilac vine (*Hardenbergia violacea* 'Happy Wanderer')

Notes

Growing a woody vine in a container garden requires a strong support. The trellis used in this scheme is anchored in the container and then to the house. The vines can take annual pruning to rein in their robust growth. Standing the container next to a porch pillar, balcony railing, or a fence gives less-vigorous vines a leg up.

BHG PLANT SWAP

ALTERNATIVE PLANTINGS

Woody vines for colder climates include climbing hydrangea, porcelain berry (*Ampelopsis*), trumpet creeper (*Campsis radicans*), and wisteria.

PART SHADE/SUN

Rising Stars

This dramatic design has a practical side too: It softens the transition from an expanse of yard to the hard, upright surfaces of walls. The large, hefty pot holds a trellis for the climbing plants and enables the striking display, even in a small area.

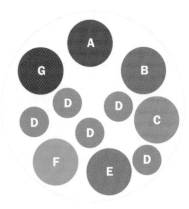

Essentials

Container: 30×12-inch watertight ceramic bowl
Materials: Pea gravel; pump-filter-fountain; small rocks or broken bricks
Light: Part shade
Water: At least 2 inches deep; deeper for water lilies

Ingredients

A. 1 violet-stemmed taro
B. 1 dwarf umbrella palm
C. 1 water lily
D. 5 water lettuce
E. 1 variegated pennywort
F. 1 horsetail
G. 1 water bluebell

Notes

Water drawn from a water softener is unsuitable to fill a potted water garden. If your water contains chlorine, letting it sit for 24 to 48 hours before planting allows the chemical to evaporate. If your water contains chloramine, you can purchase a product at garden centers to remove the chemical.

Water World

Create a pretty miniature aquascape in an afternoon. First choose a watertight container. One with a dark-color interior helps minimize algae growth. Then select from many kinds of water plants—some float, others just like to have wet feet.

Choose plants with various leaf sizes, shapes, and colors.

step 1

step 2

HERE'S HOW...

1 Set the container in place

where it will receive about 6 hours of sun daily. Rinse the gravel several times to remove residue. Cover the bottom of the pot with 2 inches of gravel. Set the pump-filter-fountain unit in place. Hide the power cord under the gravel.

2 Keep plants in pots

Use a clay-type potting soil, not a lightweight potting mix that contains fertilizer. Cover the top of the soil in each pot with a layer of gravel to hold the soil and the pot in place.

3 Set potted plants in place

Stage plants on flat rocks or broken bricks so the top edge of each pot will be at water level. Add water. Turn on the pump and adjust the fountain height. Add water daily as it evaporates. Use dunk tablets (from a garden center) when the fountain isn't running to control mosquitoes.

A 30-gallon water garden can include two or three goldfish.

step 3

Winter Wonderland

Finish the gardening season by filling a generously deep window box with festive elfin shrubs, then enjoy a cheery evergreen landscape right outside your window through the fall and winter.

Essentials

Container: 36×11×9-inch cedar window box
Light: Part shade
Water: Apply warm water when the top inch of soil feels dry

Ingredients

A. 1 dwarf cedar ('Port Orford')
B. 1 white cedar ('Sunkist')
C. 2 wintercreeper (*Euonymous* 'Emerald Gaiety')
D. 1 winter heather

E. 1 white cedar ('Rheingold')
F. 1 false cypress ('Boulevard')
G. 1 false cypress ('Elwoodii')
H. 1 false cypress ('Hinoki')

Notes

A layer of mulch slows moisture loss on sunny days. Spray an antidessicant (from a garden center) on evergreens, following product directions, to help prevent damage from winter winds.

BIG CONTAINER BASICS

READY FOR THE COLD

Make sure the dwarf conifers and other evergreens you select for your planter are winter-hardy in your area. Move the planter to a protected place, if necessary.

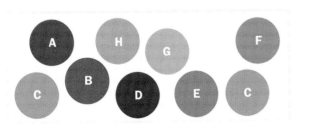

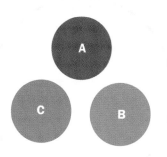

Essentials
Container: 12-inch wooden planter
Light: Part shade
Water: Keep soil damp

Ingredients
A. false cypress ('Ellwoodii')
B. creeping thyme
C. wintercreeper (*Euonymous* 'Gold Splash')

Notes
Bring the potted dwarf conifer indoors in fall and use it as a tabletop tree through the holiday season. Keep the plant in a cool room and the soil evenly damp before moving the container back outdoors in spring.

USE A COASTER
Disguise a pot saucer or tray using preserved sheet moss. It will give your container garden a more natural appearance and help protect the surface of a tabletop at the same time.

What Goes Around

A dwarf conifer provides an evergreen framework for a potted scheme. Accompanying it with other long-season green plants produces a textural composition. For special occasions, you can dress up the greenery by tucking in a small vase of colorful cut flowers.

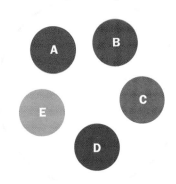

Essentials

Container: 14-inch glazed ceramic pot
Light: Part shade to shade
Water: Keep soil damp

Ingredients

A. 1 button fern
B. 1 peacock plant (*Calathea*)
C. 1 pink geranium (Martha Washington)
D. 1 rex begonia
E. 1 pink cyclamen

Notes

Keep this potted garden going year round. Between late summer and spring, place it indoors in a site where it will receive bright, indirect light. Before you let this potted garden vacation outdoors over the summer, remove the geranium from the container and transplant it into a separate pot. All the plants will have more growing room now. Set the potted garden in a place where it will not receive direct sun. Place the geranium in partly sunny spot.

BHG TEST GARDEN TIP

B REX

Rex begonias need high humidity and cool shade during the hot, dry days of summer. When growing a rex begonia on its own, set the potted plant on a large saucer or tray filled with wet gravel to boost humidity.

In the Pink

Look to houseplants for a wide selection of dramatically textured and colorful foliage. Group three or five plants with similar needs for light and water, then plant them together in a complementary pot that provides enough room for their growth.

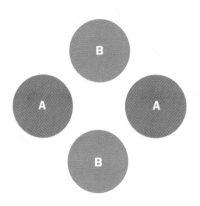

Essentials

Container: 12×12×6-inch flexible stone-veneer planter
Materials: Glass hurricane; taper candle
Light: Part shade to shade
Water: When soil begins to feel dry

Ingredients

A. 2 heuchera ('Dolce Mocha Mint')
B. 2 heuchera ('Dolce Key Lime Pie')

Notes

Choose from a new generation of heuchera—coral bells—with bold-color foliage, vigorous adaptability, and delicious-sounding names for strong additions to long-lasting container gardens. You'll find options with leaf colors including chartreuse, amber, orange, purple, and black.

BHG TEST GARDEN TIP

SUPERIOR PERENNIAL
Move the heuchera to the garden at the end of summer. The plants will adapt quickly to garden beds where they get heat and sun, but they will fare best in part shade and cool weather.

Keeping Romance Alive

Who can resist the allure of an instant garden, let alone one that conjures special effects? Plant this centerpiece in minutes, using two colors of the same plant. You'll appreciate its long-lasting beauty as well as the source of glowing candlelight on an outdoor table.

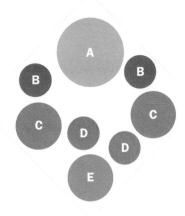

Essentials

Container: 18-inch glazed frostproof pot
Light: Part shade to shade
Water: Keep soil damp

Ingredients

A. 1 blue lacecap hydrangea
B. 2 English ivy
C. 2 leatherleaf fern
D. 2 purple viola
E. 1 chartreuse licorice plant

Notes

Tuck bright green reindeer moss (from a crafts store) in between the young plants to heighten the contrast between them and enhance the garden's overall appeal. As the plants mature, they'll gradually hide the moss.

TEST GARDEN TIP

POT ON

A hydrangea or other shrub will outgrow its container every two to three years. In early spring, before the plant resumes growth, transplant it into a larger pot to promote growth and flowering. Repot the shrub using fresh potting mix, and water it thoroughly after transplanting.

Blue Heaven

Launch the gardening season with this gorgeous scheme. Depending on where you live, start it indoors in late winter or early spring and then move it outdoors once warm weather has come to stay. In late summer transplant the hydrangea into the garden. Save the ferns for next year's container.

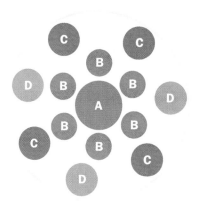

Essentials
Container: 18-inch polystyrene planter
Light: Shade
Water: Keep soil damp

Ingredients
A. 1 arborvitae
B. 6 pink impatiens
C. 4 blue-purple wishbone flower (*Torenia*)
D. 3 variegated trailing vinca ('Wojo's Jem')

Notes
Consider a polystyrene (foam) container for your next long-term potted garden. The lightweight, nonporous material will make the garden more portable, less thirsty for water, and less susceptible to temperature extremes.

BHG CAN-DO DESIGN

LEADERSHIP ROLE
It isn't necessary to place the focal-point plant in the center of a potted garden. Think about where the container will be displayed, how it will be viewed, and how the plants will best balance one another. Then plant accordingly.

All Dressed Up

Centering your potted garden design on a long-term focal point, such as a dwarf arborvitae, will take it from one season into the next for at least two years. Change the annual underplantings for spring-to-fall and fall-to-spring displays.

CHAPTER SIX

Secrets to Success

Lush, colorful container gardens start with good basic gardening techniques. **Once you learn how to give plants what they need, including quality soil, adequate water, and help in times of trouble, the rewards come easily.**

Soil

Success begins with soil. This mantra applies to all gardeners and gardens. In a container garden, the best soil provides plants with the water, nutrients, and air they need to thrive.

The ideal soil will not come from your yard—garden soil is too heavy, compacts too easily, and drains poorly in pots. Instead, the best soil is formulated to drain well but still hold moisture; it is light enough to facilitate a portable container but heavy enough to keep it from toppling over in a strong wind.

For convenience, use an all-purpose potting mix that includes a blend of ingredients, such as peat, vermiculite, perlite, sand, and bark, suited to most potted plants.

The package will tell you if it's a soilless mix (made primarily with peat, coir/coconut husk, bark, wood chips, or sawdust), which will be lightweight and dry out quickly. A soil-based mix (made with sterilized, garden-variety loam) will be heavier and hold moisture and nutrients longer.

Experiment with both types of mix and a variety of products to determine which ones work best for your plants.

Special mixes

A premium potting mix containing slow-release fertilizer and water-holding polymer crystals lessens feeding and watering but doesn't eliminate the chores. You'll save money by adding these ingredients to a standard potting mix instead.

Customize a potting mix to suit your plants' needs. For example, make an extra-sandy, well-draining blend for succulents, or an organic, compost-enriched mix for edibles. Or enrich and enhance a lightweight, peat-based mix with compost and polymer crystals, making it more moisture retentive; it will work well for plants that prefer damp soil. Use the mix in window boxes, hanging baskets, and other containers that dry out quickly.

When blending your own potting mediums, moisten the peat moss and vermiculite with warm water before adding them to the mix. Once saturated, they're easier to manage and blend with other ingredients.

Make enough potting mix to keep it on hand.

right Refresh soil in year-round containers annually by replacing the loose soil around the plants' root balls with fresh potting mix plus a dose of slow-release fertilizer.

opposite One cubic foot of potting mix will fill a container 15 inches in diameter and 12 inches deep.

These ingredients, when included in soil mixes, have specific roles. Customize a mix to suit your plants' needs for moisture and drainage using these materials, compost, sand, and other ingredients.

peat moss
This lightweight organic material soaks up water and nutrients like a sponge.

vermiculite
Flakes of mica (a mineral) expanded by heat absorb water, release it slowly, and keep soil mix porous.

perlite
Heat-expanded granules of volcanic ash do not absorb water, but help soil drain and resist compaction.

Planting

Ready: A clean or new container with adequate drainage. Set: Potting mix, fertilizer, and plants. Go: It's planting time! Your attention to details at this stage will help ensure strong, healthy plants. Use these techniques and tips to make the process more satisfying.

Plant in place if the container will be too heavy to lift and move when filled.

Before planting terra-cotta or any other porous pot type, soak it in water. A dry clay pot absorbs moisture from soil, taking water from plants.

Fill a container half to three-quarters full with potting mix. Blend in slow-release fertilizer and water-retentive crystals, if desired. Top with plain potting mix.

Arrange plants while they're still in their nursery pots. Set them in the container, starting with the largest or tallest and finishing with the smallest ones.

Place the largest plant in the center of the container for a symmetrical design; off to one side for an asymmetrical balance. Rearrange plants until you're pleased with the display.

Just before planting, dip each plant's root ball in a solution of water and root stimulator formulated for transplants (available where garden supplies are sold).

Remove one plant at a time from its nursery pot, starting with the largest. To dislodge a large plant from a nursery pot, gently lay the pot on its side and press firmly on it with your foot. Roll the pot to the opposite side and repeat the process. Then slide the plant out of the pot.

To plant, set the plant in the container and add potting mix around the root ball. Set smaller plants in place. Fill in between plants with soil mix without packing it.

If you wish to plant seeds, sow them directly in a container filled with potting mix. Follow planting instructions on seed packets.

Leave 2 inches between the top of the soil mix and the container for water and mulch.

After planting, moisten the potting mix thoroughly (until water runs out the pot's drainage hole).

THE DRAIN GAME

Every container must provide drainage, giving excess water an escape route. Placing pot shards in the bottom of a container is no longer recommended—this technique hinders drainage instead of improving it.

screen
If a container's drainage hole is large, cover it with screening, newspaper, or a coffee filter to prevent soil from leaking out.

gravel
If a container has no drainage hole and you prefer not to drill one in it, create a drainage area using a 2-inch layer of gravel.

liner
When lining a container with landscape fabric or plastic, cut drainage holes in the liner.

When planting
a container, add
enough potting
mix to place plants
near the top of the
container, keeping
them at a depth
comparable to their
nursery pots.

above Set up a planting area in the shade. After
a few days, when plants have recovered from the
initial shock of transplanting, move them to their
desired location.

left If you discover a plant's roots tightly bound
when you remove its nursery pot, gently squeeze
the root ball to loosen it and tease loose the
roots before planting.

Watering

Consistent, routine watering is vital to plants' health, especially when roots can't seek out moisture because they're confined.

Containers usually require watering daily during summer or every two or three days during cooler periods, unless nature handles it for you. Hot, dry weather and small pots can necessitate twice-daily watering.

Plants suffer from too much water as much as from too little. Determine if a container garden needs water by poking your finger into the soil up to the second knuckle. If the soil feels dry, it's time to water. Check pots daily.

Saturate the potting mix thoroughly. Excess water should drain away from the containers. Soil sours, roots rot, and root-killing mineral salts build up in a container that drains poorly.

If a soilless mix dries out completely, rewet it by standing the pot in a large vessel of water overnight.

Watering early in the day is best. It allows plants to soak up what they need before afternoon heat causes excessive evaporation.

Watering in the evening can leave moisture on foliage and promote disease.

Use a watering can to water only a few containers. Group pots and water them all at once.

Using drip irrigation set up on a timer takes the work out of watering. A drip system also saves water by delivering it near plants' root zones with as little evaporation and runoff as possible. Check the system seasonally, especially in hard-water areas, to make sure the timer works and lines are not clogged or punctured.

Self-watering pots feature a built-in reservoir that delivers moisture to the soil. They require watering less frequently.

Water-holding mats fit into the bottom of hanging baskets and other containers, wicking moisture into the soil.

below left Water-holding polymer crystals absorb moisture and dissolved nutrients, then gradually deliver them to plants' roots as needed. Add crystals to potting mix before planting.

below right Collect and use rainwater on plants whenever possible. Plants will be affected if the water supply at your home is hard (contains mineral salts) or softened.

Hand-watering with an adjustable sprayer attached to a garden hose helps control the flow with less waste and directs water into the soil instead of on foliage.

IRRIGATION MADE EASY

A simple-to-install drip irrigation system can be customized to suit your garden and target your thirstiest plants.

drip irrigation
A drip system supplies water to containers via tubes branching from a main line.

emitter
Place one emitter—attached to flexible tubing—in each container, even a hanging basket.

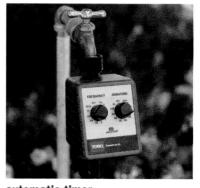

automatic timer
An automatic timer turns a drip irrigation system on and off, handling the job for you.

Feeding

High-performance plants need nutrients to produce vigorous foliage and bright blooms. Regular fertilizing helps keep container plants healthy because frequent watering flushes important nutrients out of the soil.

Gradual-release plant food, blended into a potting mix before planting, offers an easy way to feed container plants continuously. The coated granules release nutrients slowly, usually over three to nine months, depending on the product.

If you use a standard potting mix that does not already include fertilizer, add gradual-release fertilizer according to package directions. Additional granules can be scratched into the soil mix later as a nutritional boost, if needed.

Water soluble plant food is an alternative. Make a solution of plant food and water, sprinkle it on the soil, and reapply it regularly throughout the growing season.

The plant food label indicates—in a series of numbers separated by dashes—the balance of the major nutrients it supplies: nitrogen-phosphorous-potassium. An all-purpose, 14-14-14 fertilizer gives plants the primary nutrients they need to thrive.

Some plants need feeding more often, including those in close quarters or in a soilless mix, as well as vigorous growers.

Edible plants and long-term plantings benefit from organic fertilizers that enrich soil and improve its structure. Organic fertilizers include compost, rotted manure, fish emulsion, and kelp products.

Plants show signs of nutrient deficiency particularly in their foliage, alerting you to their need for fertilizer. Clues include pale or discolored leaves, weak or slow growth, and smaller leaves and flowers.

Taper off plant food as the end of the gardening season approaches.

above right Terra-cotta and unglazed earthenware pots leach fertilizer out of soil faster than plastic or glazed pots. Plants in porous pots will need to be fed more often.

right Give plants a boost at planting time with a water-soluble transplant fertilizer.

Follow package directions when using fertilizer. Feeding more than the recommended amount can harm plants.

Mulching

Mulch is a funny word, but the stuff has a serious job. As it covers the surface of the potting mix in your container gardens, the layer of loose material works primarily to conserve soil moisture. Mulching is not necessary, but it benefits your garden and you in more ways as well.

Mulch prevents soil from washing out of pots and splashing on foliage when you water plants.

Mulch also insulates soil and plant roots, helping them keep cooler during the hottest days of summer.

Organic mulches, such as cocoa shells and chipped or shredded bark, decompose gradually and add to the soil mix. Ornamental mulches, including pebbles, shells, and recycled glass, are effective mulching materials as well as pretty.

Mulch deters squirrels, slugs, and other critters from pestering container plantings. Squirrels won't bother digging in gravel or medium- to large-bark mulch. Slugs will avoid any gritty mulch.

How to mulch

In spring, after rain or watering, top the soil with a 1- to 2-inch layer of mulch. Apply it loosely and evenly; avoid compacting mulch and piling it up around plant stems.

Take advantage of the ornamental value that comes with many mulches. Crushed recycled glass, polished river stones, marbles, and flat glass drops come in a multitude of colors. They glisten when wet and reflect sunlight. Terra-cotta spheres and seashells are especially eyecatching.

Mix and match plants and mulches to find the most effective and pleasing combinations. For example, organic nutshells and fragrant cocoa shells work especially well in edible gardens; herbs and alpines have a proclivity for fine gravel.

left and opposite Topdress container plantings with pea gravel or another mulch that helps hold in soil moisture and provides a neat finishing touch.

recycled glass

cocoa shells

seashells

terra-cotta spheres

Grooming

It takes just a few minutes a day to keep container gardens healthy and vigorous. Combining grooming and watering in a routine also gives you an opportunity to spot any disease or pest problems early. Follow these steps to accomplish basic maintenance of your plants.

Deadheading

Remove flowers as soon as they begin to shrivel, fade, or otherwise appear spent.

Use your fingers or pruners to pinch off spent flowers. This also helps prevent annuals from completing their life cycle and producing seeds.

While you're at it, remove any discolored or damaged foliage.

Pruning

Snip back fast-growing or untidy plants that show signs of unruliness or unattractive bare stems.

Trim a plant for a better shape in graceful proportion to the container and any planting companions.

Prevent annuals from becoming scraggly or overgrown by midsummer, trimming 1 to 2 inches from them every other week. If plants become scraggly and bloom less, cut them back by one-third to one-half; then fertilize the plants and watch them rebound quickly.

Replanting

By late summer or early fall, when some plants have passed their peak and appear bedraggled, it is time to replace them. Use a hand trowel to carefully lift a declining plant from the container and replace it with a new one.

Long-term plantings need rejuvenating too. After two or three years, remove the tree, shrub, or perennial from the pot. Trim as much as one-third of the larger roots, especially those circling the root ball or tangled in tight masses. Loosen the root ball. Replant in a pot at least 2 inches larger with fresh potting mix.

Pests & diseases

Look for signs of pests or diseases, such as disfigured or discolored foliage or visible insect pests. Take action right away.

Diagnose the problem accurately before taking steps to remedy it.

Handpick insects or blast them off with forceful water from a garden hose. Remove and discard affected plant parts.

below left Revitalize plants with weak growth by lifting them from the pot, loosening the roots, replacing the potting mix, and replanting.
below Deadheading entails pinching or cutting off flowers that have finished blooming.

After

A quick makeover
revives a tired
container. A dying
geranium and spindly
petunias (below) are
removed, leaving a
healthy New Zealand
flax. Then African
daisy, heuchera 'Dolce
Key Lime Pie', and
wood spurge 'Efanthia'
are added to refresh
the planting (left).

Before

Pot Holders

Giving your container garden a lift—literally raising it off the ground—has practical advantages. First, good drainage is crucial. If excess water cannot escape from a container or becomes trapped under it, plant roots will suffocate, die, and rot. Second, if your container sits on a deck, balcony, or comparable surface, drainage may be impeded and the surface might be stained or damaged by moisture.

Pot feet add to the decorative charm of a container garden. Elevating a pot using pot feet raises it enough to facilitate drainage. Using pot feet also allows air circulation under the pot and prevents staining of the surface beneath.

Placing a saucer under a pot catches excess water and helps prevent surface staining too. Pour excess water out of a saucer—only some water garden plants benefit from standing with their roots submerged.

If a pot lacks a drainage hole and drilling one isn't an option, use it as a cachepot—a decorative holder—instead. Set a planted pot in it, elevating the inner pot with a 2-inch layer of gravel, pot shards, or styrene packing materials to allow drainage. Empty any excess water occasionally.

Set the stage

Showcase your container gardens by staging them at different levels for greater appeal.

Choose a plant stand that will weather the elements outdoors. A stand with multiple shelves and a tiered design enables you to display a variety of containers and even store gardening tools.

Make sure elevated containers are stable. Beware of placing large or heavy containers on the highest shelf of a tiered stand, making it top-heavy. A tall or tiered plant stand may need to be anchored to an adjoining wall to stabilize it.

Match the accessory to the task. The extra weight of an iron plant stand or an anchored plant shelf can help keep a pot upright on a windy day.

right An iron plant stand uses vertical space to display a collection of small pots. The arrangement makes it easy to tend the garden.

left A tall plant stand provides a decorative means of displaying small container gardens and keeping them within easy reach.

below Pot feet promote plant health by lifting containers enough to allow excess water to drain away easily and letting more oxygen reach plant roots.

HOLD IT!

Consider an array of options for elevating your container gardens. Wrought-iron accessories prove weatherworthy and handsome.

A plant stand gives legs to a container, boosting its drainage ability as well as its visibility.

An iron pot holder, fastened to an exterior wall, secures a window-height display.

Some plant stands can move indoors and outdoors with your potted plants.

Summer & Winter Care

Planning a summer vacation? Remember your container gardens and make arrangements to help them survive while you're away for an extended period. While you're at it, think ahead to cold-season protection and safeguard your investment in plants and pots.

Plants should fare well for a long weekend as long as you leave them well watered.

Prepare for a longer getaway by grouping plants close together, out of direct sun and wind (under the eaves of the house or garage, for instance).

Ask a neighbor or friend to check on your container gardens while you're away and water if necessary.

Set pots on a 1-inch layer of stones or gravel inside large saucers or tubs. Pour water into each reservoir until it reaches the pot's bottom.

Remove fading flowers and harvest mature and nearly-ripe vegetables and fruits to reduce the drain on plants' resources.

Plan way ahead: At planting time use self-watering containers, drought-resistant plants, and moisture-holding crystals in your potting mix. Your container gardens will be less dependent on you for water.

Cold-season protection

Where freezing weather threatens plants, protect them and your pots from the ravages of winter.

Most containers will be at risk if left outdoors unprotected during winter. Moisture from rain or snow held in a pot can freeze, expand, and crack or break the vessel.

Weatherproof containers such as resin or plastic can be left outdoors year round, but they require good drainage to complete their job effectively.

Before planting a year-round pot, line it with bubble wrap to help protect the container from damage caused by wet potting soil freezing, expanding, and pressing on it.

below Myriad watering kits with timers, such as the Green Genius system, work while you're on vacation.

below right Leave well-watered potted plants in a shaded place with saucers under them.

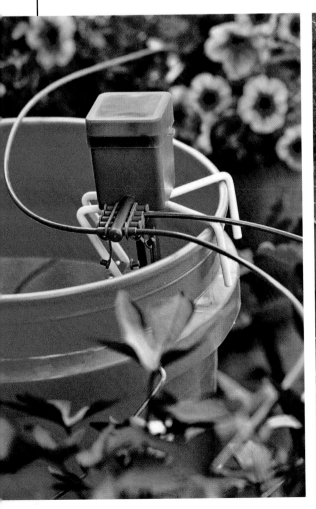

Move containers off a deck or other exposed site and set them in garage, shed, or more sheltered part of the landscape.

In Zones 4 and colder:
Move tender plants indoors for the winter.
Save valuable trees, shrubs, and perennials by lifting them from containers and transplanting them into the garden in late summer or early fall.

In Zones 5, 6, and 7:
Protect potted trees and shrubs by wrapping the pot and plant in a winter coat made using layers of bubble wrap and burlap, and secured with twine.
Keep the soil mix slightly damp throughout the winter months.

above Snow-filled pots look pretty, but this is one of the worst ways to leave them at the end of the gardening season. They'll be vulnerable to damage from frost, ice, and freeze-thaw cycles.
right Glass watering mushrooms or globes slowly drip water to plants' root zones.

Portable Pots

Large, bulky pots can be heavy, especially when filled with soil and plants. Use these tips to lighten the load and move pots more easily without injuring yourself.

Plan for mobility. Take advantage of lightweight and portable containers. Made of polystyrene, resin, or fiberglass, they resemble heavier terra-cotta, stone, or concrete.

Choose a lightweight potting mix, especially when the container's weight poses an issue, such as a larger or permanent planter on a balcony or rooftop.

Lightweight pots and tall containers with narrow bottoms need a weighted base to stabilize them and prevent tipping.

Lighten a large container by reducing its volume. Fill the bottom third (or less) of it with styrene packing pieces secured in a plastic shopping bag.

Placing bricks or large stones in the bottom of a lightweight container will help stabilize it but won't improve its mobility.

If you can't lift a potted planting, it's probably too heavy to place on a railing, bracket, or hook.

Move it!

Rolling plant stands and other caddies with casters make moving heavy containers a breeze. Plant caddies also keep excess water from damaging the surface beneath them.

Casters roll easily across a hard surface. Move a pot across ground, gravel, or another soft surface by sliding a tarp or sheet of heavy-duty plastic under the container and dragging it.

Move container gardens before—not after—watering.

above right Sliding a pot around on a patio, deck, or other hard surface can mar the surface and damage the pot. Use plant stands on casters or caddies to avoid problems.

right A large, seasonal container requires less potting mix if you fill the bottom of it with pinecones, plastic water bottles, or overturned nursery cell packs.

above Use the leverage of a two-wheel dolly or hand truck to shift and cart hefty pots.

left Keep an eye out for new products that make container gardening easier. This pot lifter is one example. It turns the chore of hoisting a heavy pot into a quick and easy task for two.

Clean & Tidy

An efficient workspace, where you can store clean pots as well as other potting supplies, makes it easier to plant and maintain container gardens.

A well-equipped potting bench fulfills a gardener's fantasies by keeping essential gear organized, within easy reach, and tidy.

Built at counter height, a potting bench provides a sturdy work surface that doesn't require you to stoop or crouch while planting. A bench with shelves above and below the work surface makes an efficient arrangement.

If a potting bench includes a small sink or other water source, it makes cleanup a snap.

A high-quality, well-constructed bench made of cedar or other weather-resistant wood that's screwed or bolted together will last longer than pine or another bargain model.

Place your potting bench in a sheltered area, under an eave or in a garage or shed.

A small outbuilding dedicated to potting plants provides a useful asset in any garden.

Build a potting shed or bench using plans, a kit, or the services of a carpenter. Or find ready-made options available from building supply stores, mail order sources, and online vendors.

Clean, oh clean

Use a stiff brush to clean pots. A wire brush helps remove mineral deposits and stains, but it can scratch and ruin some pots. A scouring pad made for kitchen or grill cleaning can scrub without scratching. Test any scrubber on the pot's bottom first to see if it scratches.

Use a splash of white vinegar on a scrubber to remove white, crusty mineral deposits on clay or other porous pots.

Use a sprinkle of baking soda on a plastic scrubber to scour synthetic pots.

Disinfect pots by soaking them for 24 hours in a solution of 9 parts water, 1 part bleach, and a squirt of liquid dish detergent; and then scrub.

below left Fall cleanup includes emptying and cleaning containers before storing them. When the gardening season returns in spring, you'll be ready to grow with clean pots.

below right A garden carryall—whether a repurposed vintage milk bottle carrier like the one shown, or a bucket, or another holder—keeps hand tools and other supplies handy and portable.

left A stiff brush helps remove soil and debris, preventing the spread of disease to new plants.

above Ideally, your potting area will be located within convenient reach of garden areas and sheltered from afternoon sun.

CHAPTER SEVEN

Plant Directory

Explore the array of plants particularly adaptable to life in containers. Mix and match your selections, depending on your garden conditions and plans.

An expansive world of wonderful plants awaits intrepid container gardeners. As you plan your container gardens and purchase plants, turn to this list to find favorites for sun, shade, and situations in between. Whether you depend on tried-and-true varieties or prefer to experiment with new and improved ones, use this guide to grow them successfully.

African daisy
(Osteospermum ecklonis)
Annual except in Zones 9–11
6–20 inches tall; 6–15 inches wide
Upright or trailing growth habit
African daisy packs a vibrant punch in hues of pink, purple, yellow, and orange. Blooms may look like typical daisies or be quilled or spoon-shape. Drought-tolerant, the plant can handle partial shade. Heat stalls flowering, and the flowers of some varieties close at night or in cloudy weather. Keep plants well watered; fertilize monthly.

Agapanthus
(Agapanthus spp.)*
Perennial in Zones 7–11
2–3 feet tall; 2 feet wide
Mounded growth habit
Throughout summer, globes of trumpet-shape bluish-purple or white flowers rise above arching, strappy evergreen leaves. They add exotic flair whether combined with other plants in the container or on their own. Plants bloom best when they are slightly rootbound and kept evenly moist. Grow them in part shade in hot climates. Overwinter plants indoors in cold climates.

Ageratum
(Ageratum houstonianum)
Annual except in Zones 9–10
Most varieties 6–12 inches tall and wide
Mounding growth habit
Also called flossflower, ageratum displays clusters of fluffy flowers in shades of purple, blue, or white all summer. Ageratum does best in rich, moist soil. To avoid disease problems, water in the morning so that leaves dry quickly. Provide afternoon shade in hot-summer climates. If a plant becomes leggy in midsummer, shear it back by half.

Angelonia
(Angelonia angustifolia)
Annual except in Zones 10–11
2–3 feet tall; 1 foot wide
Upright growth habit
Also known as summer snapdragon, angelonia blooms reliably all summer with spires of intense blue, purple, pink, white, or a mix of these colors. Place angelonia at the center or back of a container. Deadhead to encourage more blooms. Plants stand up to extended heat and humidity, even in southern climates. Slightly moist soil is best.

Bacopa
(Sutera hybrids)*
Annual except in Zones 9–11
4–12 inches long and wide
Trailing growth habit
Small, delicate flowers on cascading stems give bacopa star power at the edge of window boxes and hanging baskets. The most popular varieties have white flowers, but pink, light blue, and lavender are also available. Heat and drought can take a toll on flowering, so sustain bacopa by growing it in part shade and keeping soil consistently moist, especially during hot, dry periods.

Black-eyed susan vine
(Thunbergia alata)
Annual
8 feet long; 2 feet wide
Trailing or climbing vine
Dark-eyed, vibrant yellow, orange, or white flowers nestle among black-eyed susan vine's soft green leaves. Support this clambering vine with a trellis to put its height to work, or let it cascade from the container. Regular watering is key to sustaining the plant's vigorous growth. Give plants an occasional trim to boost flowering.

Calibrachoa
(*Calibrachoa* hybrids)
Annual
8–12 inches long; 4–6 inches wide
Trailing and mounding types
Consistent performance and colorful blooms in shades of yellow, red, white, pink, and purple make calibrachoa ideal for containers. These low-maintenance superstars resist disease and require no deadheading. Mounding varieties work well tucked among other plants; trailers are best at edges. Plants tolerate part shade, but flowering is reduced.

Cuphea
(*Cuphea* spp.)
Annual except in Zones 9–11
1–1½ feet tall; 1 foot wide
Mounded growth habit
This group of species thrives in heat and humidity. Cigar plant (*C. ignea*), is bushy with slender, tubular, black-tipped red flowers. Mexican heather (*C. hyssopifolia*) forms a dense mound of lavender blooms. Bat-face cuphea (*C. llavea*) has flared tubular blooms in red and purple. For all, keep soil moist, but avoid overwatering; pinch tips to encourage bushiness.

Dahlia
(*Dahlia* hybrids)
Tuberous roots; perennial in Zones 8–11
1–6 feet tall; 1–3 feet wide
Upright growth habit
Dahlias boast petal-packed flowers in bright shades of pink, red, yellow, orange, purple, and white that are excellent for cutting. Grow them in mixed plantings or alone in their own pots. Feed plants every two weeks; cut flowers to promote branching. Dahlias grow from tuberous roots. In winter store them indoors in a cool, dry place to protect the tuberous roots from frost.

Dusty miller
(*Senecio cineraria*)
Annual except in Zones 8–11
1–2 feet tall and wide
Upright growth habit
Grown for its silvery, fernlike foliage, dusty miller works well with other plants to set off their colors and textures in mixed containers. This workhorse keeps on through intense heat and drought, but does best when watered every other day and fed monthly. Snip off flower spikes to keep growth compact.

Elephant's ear
(*Colocasia* spp.)
Tuber; perennial in Zones 9–11
2–4 feet tall; 2–3 feet wide
Upright growth habit
This large, dramatic accent makes a good backdrop for other container plantings. Its heart-shape green to purple leaves arise from a tuber. The larger the tuber, the bigger and bolder the foliage. Elephant's ear thrives in rich, moist to wet soil and can be planted in water. Before the first frost bring the container inside for winter; let the plant rest by placing it in subdued light and watering minimally.

Fan flower
(*Scaevola aemula*)
Annual except in Zones 10–11
8–12 inches long; 6 inches wide
Trailing form
Named for its fan-shape purple, blue, pink, or white blooms, this Australian import is prized for heat tolerance and summerlong flowering. Plant it at a pot's edge to take advantage of the cascading habit. Keep soil evenly moist but avoid overwatering. Feed plants weekly. Cut back leggy stems to encourage branching and continuous bloom.

Fountain grass
(Pennisetum spp.)
Perennial (Zones 5–9) and annual
1–4 feet tall; 1½–3 feet wide
Arching growth habit
With its feathery plumes amid dense clumps of graceful blades, fountain grass adds texture and movement to containers. It's spectacular alone or combined with colorful plants such as pentas or lantana. Plants can reach 4 feet but rarely grow that tall in pots. Look for annual fountain grass (*P. setaceum* 'Rubrum') or perennial (*P. alopecuroides*). Keep soil moist.

Geranium
(Pelargonium × *hortorum)*
Annual except in zones 9–11
1–2 feet tall and wide
Mounding growth habit
Geraniums bloom from spring through fall with single or double flowers in a range of hues. Fancy-leaf varieties offer intriguing variegated markings. Easy-to-grow geraniums need regular deadheading and feeding; pinch stems to maintain the desired shape. They also thrive in part shade but not high heat and humidity. Trailing ivy geraniums (*P. peltatum*) suit hanging baskets and pot edges.

Gloriosa daisy
(Rudbeckia hirta)
Short-lived perennial in Zones 4–9
1–3 feet tall; 1 foot wide
Upright growth habit
A member of the black-eyed susan family, gloriosa daisy is showier than its cousins, boasting large, brightly colored, dark-eyed blooms in shades of red, orange, or yellow. Heat and drought tolerant, these robust growers flower from June through September with regular deadheading. 'Irish Eyes', 1½ to 2 feet tall, sports yellow flowers with green centers.

Helenium
(Helenium spp.)
Perennial (Zones 4–8) and annual
1–5 feet tall; 1–1½ feet wide
Upright (perennials) or mounded (annual)
growth habit
Heleniums are nontraditional choices for late-summer to fall containers. Starting in mid-July, perennial varieties light up the pot with yellow, red, bronze, or orange blossoms that attract butterflies. For seasonal containers, try perennial helenium (*H. autumnale*) or the annual 'Dakota Gold'.

Hibiscus
(Hibiscus spp.)
Perennial (Zones 5–9) and annual
2–6 feet tall; 2–3 feet wide
Upright, shrubby growth habit
Chinese hibiscus (*H. rosa-sinensis*) blooms prolifically in show-stopping colors from summer through fall. Garden centers often sell it trained into tall standards. Bring the tender tropical plants indoors for winter. Hardy hibiscus (*H. moscheutos*) showcases larger and stunning blooms. Both types of hibiscus attract hummingbirds. Deadhead plants to ensure continued bloom.

Kale and ornamental cabbage
(Brassica oleracea)
Annual
12–15 inches tall and wide
Mounding growth habit
Kale and ornamental cabbage's rosettes of green, blue-green, white, purple, or vibrant red edible leaves accent cool-season container plantings. The main difference between the two is that ornamental cabbage grows into a tight head while kale forms a loose one. Both perform best in the cool temperatures of spring and fall; they become gangly and weak in warm temperatures.

Lantana
(*Lantana spp.* and hybrids)
Annual except in Zones 7–11
10–40 inches tall; 20 inches wide
Cascading, upright, or mounded growth habit
Lantana's bold blooms in purple, red, pink, yellow, orange, white, and mixed-colors attract butterflies. Plants bloom best with light feeding, daily watering, and deadheading; they tolerate hot, dry conditions, high humidity, and light shade. Varieties have varying growth habits. To encourage branching, pinch stem tips.

Licorice plant
(*Helichrysum petiolare*)
Annual except in Zones 9–10
6–12 inches long and wide
Stiffly trailing growth habit
Choose licorice plant for cascading charm. The species has furry silvery green foliage; cultivars include chartreuse ('Limelight' and 'Lemon') as well as variegated cream-and-green ('Licorice Splash') and white-and-green ('Variegata'). Licorice plants are vigorous growers that can overtake their companions, so be prepared to cut them back. Most need full sun. Feed plants monthly.

Marguerite daisy
(*Argyranthemum frutescens*)
Annual except in Zones 9–11
1–2 feet tall and wide
Mounding growth habit
Marguerite daisy produces a profusion of dainty yellow-centered blossoms in shades of yellow, white, pink, or lavender. Feed lightly and deadhead regularly to keep fresh blooms coming and maintain a tidy, bushy form. Plants bloom best in cool weather; pot them in early spring, when they are available, or in summer where the climate is typically cool.

Marigold
(*Tagetes* spp.)
Annual
6–24 inches tall; 12 inches wide
Mounded or upright growth habit
Easy to grow and heat resistant, marigolds bloom from summer through fall in yellow, white, orange, or red. Consider 1- to 2-foot-tall African marigold (*T. erecta*) with large flowers; shorter and more floriferous French marigold (*T. patula*); or similarly petite signet marigold (*T. tenuifolia*), which has a pleasing scent. Marigolds need frequent deadheading and attention to avoid pest problems.

Nasturtium
(*Tropaeolum majus*)
Annual except in Zones 9–11
1–8 feet long; 2 feet wide
Trailing, climbing, or bushy form
Jewel-tone blooms of yellow, cream, apricot, and red make nasturtiums a standout in pots. A bonus: They're edible, adding a peppery zing to salads and other dishes. Nasturtium's lily padlike leaves may be solid green or speckled with white. Happiest in full sun to part shade, they grow easily from seed. Plants bloom best in cool weather and infertile soil.

Nemesia
(*Nemesia fruticans*)
Annual except in Zones 8–10
10–16 inches tall; 10 inches wide
Upright growth habit
Nemesia shines from spring through fall in hues of yellow, red, purple, pink, or white. Use it to anchor the center of a container or at the base of taller container plantings. Several varieties reseed if you fail to deadhead regularly, so you might find volunteer seedlings in the garden the following year. Water plants daily and feed them with a bloom-boosting fertilizer every two weeks.

New Zealand flax
(Phormium tenax)
Perennial in Zones 7–11
2–4 feet tall; 2 feet wide
Upright growth habit
New Zealand flax's striking, spiky foliage is often striped with white, red, bronze, orange, or yellow. The plant creates dazzling height, color, and texture in lightly shaded container gardens. Grow it alone or in the center of a large container with small mounded or cascading companions that won't overtake the slow grower. Water generously and fertilize weekly until late summer.

Pentas
(Pentas lanceolata)
Annual; perennial in Florida
1–2 feet tall and wide
Upright or mounding growth habit
Native to Africa, pentas is pretty as well as tough, lapping up hot, humid conditions. Large flower clusters bloom from early spring until frost in hues of lavender, red, white, and pink, and fit most color palettes. The pink and red varieties especially draw butterflies, birds, and hummingbirds. Deadhead regularly to promote flowering.

Petunia
(Petunia hybrids)
Annual except in Zones 10–11
6–12 inches tall; 12–36 inches wide
Mounding or trailing growth habit
When it comes to fast-growing annuals, few outpace petunias. Plant a few along the edge of your container, and they'll quickly cloak it in bloom. These vigorous growers also make charming hanging baskets. Several types are available, including cascading and mounding forms as well as large- and small-flowered varieties, with single or double blossoms.

Purple heart
(Setcreasea pallida)
Annual except in Zones 8–11
6–12 inches long; 1–3 feet wide
Trailing growth habit
Purple heart gets its name from its dark foliage. Give it star power in hanging baskets or as a container edging contrasted with taller chartreuse foliage plants. Also known as Tradescantia pallida, it produces pale pink flowers from midsummer to early fall. The plant grows best in full sun or light shade and loses its purple hue in too much shade. Fertilize once a month.

Sage and salvia
(Salvia spp.)
Annual and perennial (hardiness varies by species)
1–3 feet tall; 2–3 feet wide
Upright growth habit
Many salvias are well-suited to pots. Varieties range from 1-foot-tall annual S. farinacea with blue or white flower spikes to 3-foot-tall perennial Autumn sage (S. greggii) with red, blue, or purple, pink, or white blooms; and 1-foot-tall common sage (S. officinialis) with colorful foliage. All are heat tolerant and prefer full sun.

Snapdragon
(Antirrhinum majus)
Annual except in Zones 10–11
12–18 inches tall; 8–10 inches wide
Upright growth habit
Easy-to-grow snapdragons span the color palette from white to purple and include bicolors. Dwarf varieties grow up to 10 inches tall; 'Rocket Series' cultivars reach 4 feet. Use tall varieties as a bright backdrop for large containers and dwarf varieties to conceal leggy bases of other plants. Snapdragons perform best in moist soil. Deadhead regularly to promote bloom.

Spurge
(*Euphorbia* spp.)

Annual and perennial (hardiness varies by species)
12–18 inches tall; 10–15 inches wide
Mounded growth habit

Spurges or wood spurges captivate with eye-catching foliage and yellow, white, or orange flower bracts in spring or summer. Foliage may be chartreuse, blue-green, dark green, red or purple, or variegated with white or yellow. Annual 'Diamond Frost' offers nonstop dainty white blooms above fine-textured light green leaves. Deadhead *Euphorbias*.

Swan river daisy
(*Brachycome iberidifolia*)

Annual
6–18 inches tall; 1–3 feet wide
Mounded growth habit

Swan river daisy's delicate, lacy foliage and fragrant daisies brighten containers from summer to fall. Blue is the most familiar color, but purple, pink, yellow, and white hues are also available. An excellent choice for hanging baskets, the plants grow in neat mounds. When they become leggy, cut them back for a new spurt of growth.

Sweet potato
(*Ipomoea batatas*)

Annual except in Zones 9–11
5–10 feet long; 1–3 feet wide
Cascading growth habit

Sweet potato's striking foliage quickly cascades over a pot's edge and across the patio. It's ideal for hanging baskets and tall containers where it can drape. Prune to prevent vines from becoming leggy or overtaking neighbors. The plants like consistently moist soil and a monthly feeding. Harvest the edible tubers at the end of the season; they're surprisingly mellow in flavor.

Verbena
(*Verbena* spp.)

Annual and perennial (hardiness varies by species)
4–14 inches tall; 8–24 inches wide
Trailing or mounded growth habit

A riot of color—shades of red, purple, pink, and white—tumbles out of hanging baskets and window boxes planted with verbena. Some varieties are bushier and more upright, making them well suited for the middle of a container. This full-sun lover tolerates heat well and likes a light feeding every two weeks. Trim spent flower stems to encourage new blooms.

Zinnia
(*Zinnia* spp.)

Annual
6–30 inches tall; 8–12 inches wide
Upright growth habit

Dazzlingly diverse, zinnia shines in an array of container settings. The abundant bloomers come in a rainbow of colors—white, ivory, yellow, orange, pink, red, and green—as well as bicolors. Depending on the variety you choose, zinnias are at home at any container position. While these hardy growers tolerate heat extremely well, they should be watered regularly to boost their blooming power.

Frequent cutting or regular deadheading and a weekly feeding with a 5-10-5 fertilizer encourage continuous bloom. Zinnias are commonly beset with powdery mildew, especially in humid regions. Give plants a little distance from other plants, allow air space in between them, to help prevent this problem. Narrow-leaf zinnias (*Z. angustifolia*) are free of this disease.

Alternanthera
(*Alternanthera* spp.)
Annual except in Zones 10–11
1–3 feet tall; 1–2 feet wide
Mounded or upright growth habit
Alternanthera, also known as calico plant and joseph's coat, is grown for green, red, or purple foliage emblazoned with brilliant yellow, orange, or hot pink. The size and shape of the foliage depends on the variety. Grow in full sun or part shade. Plant this vivid grower in the middle or back of a container and keep the soil moist. Pinch regularly to prevent legginess.

Asparagus fern
(*Asparagus densiflorus*)
Annual except in Zones 9–11
2–3 feet tall; 3–4 feet wide
Arching form
Fernlike evergreen foliage and a tough nature make asparagus fern a favorite for containers, especially hanging baskets. Although not a true fern, this undemanding houseplant does best in part shade and peat-rich soil. Bring it inside for the winter. In spring, cut stems close to the soil to promote new growth and improved form.

Cupflower
(*Nierembergia* spp.)
Annual except in Zones 7–9
1 foot tall and wide
Mounding growth habit
Small cup-shape flowers in purple, lavender, blue, or white cover the arching mounds of cupflower's finely textured foliage. High heat and humidity can slow flowering. Provide afternoon shade and mulch soil to keep it cool. Plants make outstanding edgers. 'Starry Eyes' and 'Blue Mountain', with lavender flowers, are more heat and drought tolerant than other varieties.

Dichondra
(*Dichondra argentea*)
Annual except in Zones 9–11
2–6 feet long; 2 feet wide
Trailing growth habit
Dichondra's strands of small, soft fan-shape leaves create a shimmering, cascade from hanging baskets and containers. A vigorous grower, its runners can grow as long as 6 feet and branch without pinching. The varieties 'Silver Falls' and 'Emerald Falls' combine especially well with purple and pink flowers. This heat- and drought- tolerant plant prefers slightly dry soil.

English ivy
(*Hedera helix*)
Perennial in Zones 5–9
2–4 feet long; 8–12 inches wide
Vining growth habit
A woody-stemmed groundcover, English ivy trails gracefully over the edge of containers. Use the versatile vine to decorate a trellis or obelisk in a pot. Its lobed leaves may be solid green or variegated with white-and-green or green-and-yellow markings. Best grown in sun or partial shade, ivy eventually crowds out small, less-aggressive plants, so choose its companions wisely.

Fuchsia
(*Fuchsia* hybrids)
Annual except in Zones 9–11
1–3 feet tall and wide
Upright or trailing growth habit
Hummingbirds are drawn to the pendulous blooms of fuchsia. Flowers appear from summer till frost in red, purple, white, pink, or bicolors. Cascading types suit hanging baskets; upright growers shine in pots or window boxes in part shade. To boost flowering, pinch stem tips in early summer. Keep the soil moist and feed plants every two weeks with fertilizer for acid-loving plants.

Heuchera
(*Heuchera* spp.)
Perennial in Zones 4–8
8–30 inches tall; 12 inches wide
Mounding growth habit
Also known as coral bells, colorful-foliaged heucheras provide a summerlong show. You'll find plain and variegated varieties in green, chartreuse, purple, bronze, brown, silver, and red. Pretty sprays of tiny bells top the colorful mounds of foliage, although some newer varieties don't bloom. Fertilize monthly. Remove spent flower stems to prolong blooming and keep plants tidy.

Lobelia
(*Lobelia erinus*)
Annual except in Zones 9–11
3–14 inches tall; 6–12 inches wide
Mounded or trailing growth habit
Blue is the most familiar color of this prolific bloomer, but it's also available in pink, purple, and white. Mounded varieties create a tidy edging, while trailing forms look best draped over the edge of hanging baskets, pots, and window boxes. Hot weather taxes the plants, which prefer cool weather and partial shade. Lightly shear spent blooms to prompt repeat flowering.

Nicotiana
(*Nicotiana* × *sanderae*)
Annual except in Zones 9–11
1–2 feet tall; 1 foot wide
Upright growth habit
Springing from a low rosette of leaves, nicotiana heralds summer with its flowers, whether crimson, lavender, pink, white, yellow, salmon, or lime green. Grow it in sun or part shade; provide afternoon shade in hot climates. Water regularly and deadhead to encourage continued blooming. The flowers attract hummingbirds.

Pansy
(*Viola* × *wittrockiana*)
Annual except in Zones 7–11
4–12 inches tall and wide
Mounded growth habit
Spring and fall containers would seem amiss without colorful pansies. They and their more diminutive cousins, violas, bloom abundantly in cool temperatures, making them ideal for seasonal containers, even winter ones where temperatures stay above freezing. Plants struggle in hot weather, so it's best to replace them each season. Feed plants lightly every two weeks.

Plectranthus
(*Plectranthus* spp.)
Annual except in Zones 9–11
15 inches tall; 2–3 feet wide
Mounded, upright, or draping form
Plectranthus is a foliage star in hues of green, gray-green, or silver, or when it's variegated white or yellow. Plants prefer some shade. Swedish ivy, the common houseplant, is one of many in this large group; Cuban oregano is another popular variety. Pinch off stem tips to promote branching. Feed plants lightly once a month.

Sedge
(*Carex* spp.)
Perennial (hardiness varies by species)
10–12 inches tall; 10 inches wide
Upright or cascading growth habit
Tufts of graceful narrow leaves lend ornamental color, texture, and elegance to container plantings. Several varieties showcase bronze foliage that pairs well with the rich purple hues of heuchera. Others sport showy white or yellow variegated foliage. Most sedges prefer moist soil and some midday shade in hot climates. Water every other day and fertilize monthly.

Begonia
(*Begonia* spp.)
Annual except in Zones 9–11
8–24 inches tall and wide
Upright or mounded growth habit

Begonias bring welcome color to shady areas. Types include shade-loving tuberous begonias with large flowers in tropical hues, and rex begonias with showy foliage. Keep plants consistently watered and fed every two weeks. Shiny-leaf wax begonias do best in sun but handle shade. Angel wing begonias form cascading mounds of color and are also good in sunny spots.

Caladium
(*Caladium bicolor*)
Tuber, annual except in Zones 10–11
2 feet tall and wide
Upright growth habit

Large, striking leaves in green, white, pink, red, or a combination of those colors lend exotic flair to containers. Although there are sun-tolerant varieties, most caladiums are happiest in shade and need ample watering, consistently moist soil, and a monthly dose of fertilizer to thrive. Tubers can be overwintered indoors and moved outdoors once temperatures stay above 60°F.

Coleus
(*Solenostemon scutellarioides*)
Annual except in Zones 10–11
1–2 feet tall and wide
Upright growth habit

Standout foliage speckled, marbled, variegated, or blended in shades of yellow, chartreuse, green, pink, red, orange, and purple makes coleus a winning container centerpiece. Leaves may be smooth or frilled, broad or slender. Most coleus prefer a shady spot and will fade or burn in full sun. Many new varieties thrive in sunny spots, and some do well in both.

Ferns
(many species)
Perennial (hardiness varies depending on species)
6–48 inches tall; 6–24 inches wide
Upright or mounding growth habit

Graceful lacy fronds add textural intrigue—and sometimes gray-green colorations—to container plantings. Whether upright or arching, ferns make elegant companions to more colorful growers such as impatiens, begonias, and coleus. Keep plants moist and feed them with a high-nitrogen fertilizer monthly.

Impatiens
(*Impatiens walleriana*)
Annual except in Zones 10–11
1 foot tall and wide
Mounding growth habit

These shade garden staples brighten pots with an array of colors. Double-flowering varieties resemble tiny roses, but the blooms drop quickly. Larger-flower New Guinea impatiens (*I. hawkeri*) convey tropical flair and perform well in sun and part shade. Impatiens wilt rapidly in hot weather; frequent watering is a must. When plants are young, pinch branch tips to encourage bushy growth.

Moneywort
(*Lysimachia nummularia*)
Perennial in Zones 3–10
1–2 feet long; 2 feet wide
Trailing growth habit

Moneywort forms a dense green mat that cascades over the edges of containers. Bright yellow cup-shape blooms emerge in summer to fall. 'Aurea' has chartreuse foliage. Although plants may bloom, the foliage packs the biggest punch with this creeping beauty. Moneywort requires consistently moist soil to look its best.

Oxalis
(Oxalis spp.)
Bulb, perennial in Zones 7–10
6–16 inches tall; 10–14 inches wide
Mounded growth habit
Also known as shamrock plant and wood sorrel, oxalis features a trio of heart-shape green or purple leaves that may be marked with black or silver. The plants also produce tiny flowers in shades of white, lavender, or yellow, depending on cultivar. Most oxalis thrive in shade or partial shade, but annual 'Molten Lava' needs full sun to showcase its orange foliage and becomes a brilliant chartreuse with more shade.

Persian shield
(Strobilanthes dyerianus)
Annual except in Zones 9–10
1½–3 feet tall; 1½–2 feet wide
Upright growth habit
Persian shield's purple foliage shimmers with hints of green and silver on top, while the leaves' underside is solid maroon. Use this lofty grower to add height to a pot. Pinch flowering stems regularly to keep growth bushy. Persian shield overwinters well on windowsills, so bring it inside when temperatures dip below 50°F outdoors. In cool regions, plants tolerate more sun.

Polka-dot plant
(Hypoestes phyllostachya)
Annual except in Zones 10–11
10–12 inches tall; 9 inches wide
Mounding growth habit
The foliage is speckled with white, red, or pink. The plant thrives in cramped quarters and humid conditions, preferring moist, rich soil. Water every other day and give a monthly feeding. Polka-dot plant has a tendency to get leggy, especially in deep shade. To encourage tidy growth, pinch stem tips, remove the flower spikes, and provide morning sun.

Spotted dead nettle
(Lamium maculatum)
Perennial in Zones 4–8
6–12 inches tall and wide
Spreading growth habit
A fast-growing groundcover, spotted dead nettle makes a showy statement spilling over the sides of a container. Most cultivars feature silver-, white-, or yellow-variegated leaves. Plants bloom in pink, lavender, or white in late May to early summer. After the first bloom, cut stems back to encourage more compact growth and avoid self sowing. Plants will take more sun in cool climates.

Vinca
(Vinca minor)
Perennial in Zones 4–11
3 feet long; 6 inches wide
Trailing growth habit
Vinca is a fast-growing groundcover prized as a trailer for pots. In spring, it unveils 1-inch-wide funnel-shape lavender or white flowers. The leaves of variegated types combine light and dark green, white, or yellow. Vinca does best in part shade. Prune regularly to keep in check; stems that reach the ground will root. Some vincas sold for pots are the species *Vinca major*, which is hardy only to Zone 7.

Wishbone flower
(Torenia spp.)
Annual except in Zones 10–11
6–12 inches tall and wide
Mounded or trailing growth habit
Peek inside the two-lipped flowers and you'll see where the name comes from. From planting to frost wishbone plant highlights shady areas with a profusion of pink, white, lavender, or purple blooms. These undemanding heat- and humidity-tolerant plants maintain a glorious show without deadheading. Feed every two weeks with a potassium-rich fertilizer.

Zone Map

USDA Plant Hardiness Zone Map

This map of climate zones helps you select plants for your garden that will survive a typical winter in your region. The United States Department of Agriculture (USDA) developed the map, basing the zones on the lowest recorded temperatures across North America. Zone 1 is the coldest area and Zone 11 is the warmest.

Plants are classified by the coldest temperature and zone they can endure. For example, plants hardy to Zone 6 survive where winter temperatures drop to –10°F, while those hardy to Zone 8 die long before it's that cold. These plants may grow in colder regions but must be brought indoors over the winter or replaced each year. Plants rated for a range of hardiness zones can usually survive winter in the coldest region as well as tolerate the summer heat of the warmest one.

To find your hardiness zone, note the approximate location of your community on the map, then match the color band marking that area to the key.

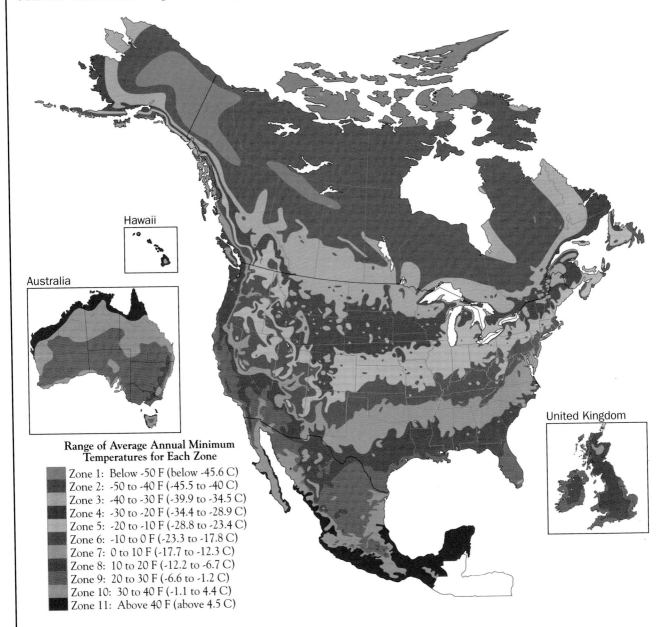

Hawaii

Australia

United Kingdom

Range of Average Annual Minimum Temperatures for Each Zone

Zone 1: Below -50 F (below -45.6 C)
Zone 2: -50 to -40 F (-45.5 to -40 C)
Zone 3: -40 to -30 F (-39.9 to -34.5 C)
Zone 4: -30 to -20 F (-34.4 to -28.9 C)
Zone 5: -20 to -10 F (-28.8 to -23.4 C)
Zone 6: -10 to 0 F (-23.3 to -17.8 C)
Zone 7: 0 to 10 F (-17.7 to -12.3 C)
Zone 8: 10 to 20 F (-12.2 to -6.7 C)
Zone 9: 20 to 30 F (-6.6 to -1.2 C)
Zone 10: 30 to 40 F (-1.1 to 4.4 C)
Zone 11: Above 40 F (above 4.5 C)

Resources

Containers

A RUSTIC GARDEN
www.arusticgarden.com
866.514.2733

BLOOM MASTER PLANTER CORP.
www.bloommaster.com
866.812.5324

CAMPANIA INTERNATIONAL, INC.
www.campaniainternational.com

HOOKS AND LATTICE
www.hooksandlattice.com
800.896.0978; 760.603.0888

SOUTHERN PATIO
www.southernpatio.com
800.729.5033

Gardening accessories & tools

GARDENER'S SUPPLY CO.
www.gardeners.com
800.876.5520

GOODS FOR THE GARDEN
www.goodsforthegarden.com
800.663.3158

GREEN GENIUS WATERING SYSTEM
Horizen Hydroponics
www.hhydro.com
866.791.1664

KINSMAN CO.
www.kinsmangarden.com
800.733.4146

LEE VALLEY TOOLS
www.leevalleytools.com
800.267.8735; from Canada: 800.267.8761

MAGNIMOIST LINERS
http://www.thinkmint.net/liners/html
800.713.6188

POTLIFTER, INC.
www.potlifter.com
888.644.4222

Plant materials

ANNIE'S ANNUALS
www.anniesannuals.com
888.266.4370

BONNIE PLANTS
www.bonnieplants.com

BRENT AND BECKY'S BULBS
www.brentandbeckysbulbs.com
877.661.2852

EASY ELEGANCE ROSES
www.easyelegancerose.com

FERNLEA
www.fernlea.com

FLOWER CARPET ROSES
www.tesselaar.com/plants/flowercarpetroses/

MONROVIA
Monrovia plants at fine garden centers nationwide. Visit www.monrovia.com to find a retailer near you.

PARK SEED CO.
www.parkseed.com
800.213.0076

PROVEN SELECTIONS AND PROVEN WINNERS
www.provenwinners.com

RENEE'S GARDEN SEEDS
www.reneesgardenseeds.com
888.880.7228

STAR ROSES
www.starroses.com

Index

Index

Index